THERE IS ONLY ONE RAFFLES

The Story of a
Grand Hotel

ILSA SHARP

This edition published by
SOUVENIR PRESS
for
Times Publishing Bhd

Copyright © 1981 Ilsa Sharp

First published 1981 by Souvenir Press Ltd,
43 Great Russell Street, London WC1B 3PA
and simultaneously in Canada
Reprinted 1982

All Rights Reserved. No part of this publication
may be reproduced, stored in a retrieval system,
or transmitted, in any form or by any means, electronic,
mechanical, photocopying, recording or otherwise without
the prior permission of the Copyright owner

ISBN 0 285 62383 4

Filmset in Great Britain by
Photobooks (Bristol) Ltd,
Barton Manor, St. Philips, Bristol

Printed in Singapore by Times Printers Sdn. Bhd.

DEDICATION

For my Mother and Father, Diana and Sam Davies,
who have lived through a war and put up with a lot from me

CONTENTS

	Introduction	9
1	The Stage is Set	12
2	The Founders	22
3	The Dancing Years	38
4	Samurai in the Palm Court	48
5	Entertaining the Guests	60
6	Behind the Scenes: the Managers	76
7	Behind the Scenes: the Staff	87
8	The 'Club'	96
9	Epicurean Food and Drink	116
10	Facing the Future	124
	Appendix: Recipes from the Raffles	135
	Selective Bibliography	139
	Acknowledgements	141

Note: All dollars in the text are Singapore dollars, unless otherwise stated.

INTRODUCTION

This is the story of one of the most famous hotels in the world. There are a number of hotels whose names have become virtually synonymous with the cities in which they are located; none however springs to mind quite so readily as does the Raffles in Singapore.

On casually overhearing a conversational reference to "Raffles" without catching the context, one could wager, with a more than even chance of winning, that the topic under discussion was the subject of these pages, rather than either the petty lotteries beloved of those responsible for church fund-raising activities, or the "gentleman burglar" who figured as the eponymous hero of E. W. Hornung's one-time best selling novel. Nowhere outside Singapore have the vicissitudes of a hotel and its birthplace been more closely interwoven. Several

Raffles Hotel—c. 1905. From *Twentieth Century Impressions of British Malaya* edited by Arnold Wright and H. A. Cartwright, 1908.

Cartoon by Denis Santry, from *Straits Produce*, April 1, 1922. Two caricature dumb-Malays are seen asking "Siapa itu?" in Malay ("Who is that?") in respect of the famous statue of Singapore's founder, Sir Stamford Raffles, and concluding that it must be a statue of "Tuan Sarkies" ("Master Sarkies"), founder of the hotel.
By courtesy of the Library of the Royal Commonwealth Society

novelists have capitalised on the dramatic potential of life behind the scenes in an international hotel by building an imaginary one and peopling it with fictional characters. But unlike their books, this one sets out to prove the essential verity of the trite saying that truth is stranger than fiction. For Raffles is a real place and all the characters—managers, staff, guests—who appear herein are real people: the men and women who took part in the creation of the worldwide Raffles legend.

Named after Sir Stamford Raffles, founder of the one-time British colony which is now the independent island state of Singapore, the Raffles was built more than a decade before the turn of the nineteenth century and came to epitomise the type of life led by the expatriate British of the colonial era. The rubber planters of the Straits Settlements and Malaya spent their leisure there, seeking in its famous Long Bar and luxurious dining and billiard rooms relief from the monotony of their lonely lives in their jungle-cleared habitats. And it has been the haunt for decades of the captains and the kings of many lands, of business tycoons as well as international rogues and adventurers, of politicians, stage and movie stars, authors and journalists.

The visiting writers, who included such famous novelists and playwrights as Rudyard Kipling, Somerset Maugham and Noel Coward, as well as a host of foreign correspondents representing the press of many countries, fed in story, song and verse, the growing store of fact and fiction that clung to the place. Through their pens, the Long Bar—birthplace of the celebrated Singapore gin sling that became the rage long before most cocktails were invented—, the Palm Court, the luxurious bathrooms, dining rooms and billiard room became familiar to thousands who had never set foot outside their native lands.

For the best part of a century, Raffles of Singapore has enjoyed a reputation founded on its "Britishness". It has been regarded as a very symbol of the old colonial Raj—as a monument to a way of life, now departed for ever, that is cherished by those who bemoan the passing of Britain's former imperial glory and derided by egalitarian critics of a later era but accorded, even by them, a sneaking admiration for its flair and *élan*.

The flavour and tradition of an *ancien régime* have remained with the Raffles throughout the years; they are in fact part of its stock in trade, but successive astute managements—starting with its non-British originators—have not allowed time to stand still. They have kept pace with every modern advance in the quality of service offered by the great chains of international hostelries and today their own landmark is as celebrated as ever for its elegant luxury, international cuisine and attentive service. The history and the fable are just an added bonus.

Raffles' situation astride the trade and tourist routes to the Far East and Australasia is a virtual guarantee that the glories of the past will be maintained for the foreseeable future.

1 THE STAGE IS SET

The stage for Raffles Hotel was set, the script almost written, in the Singapore of the 1880s. The British colony was then frontier country where a few lonely pioneer whites beavered away, in the comforting shade of the British flag, with the hordes of Asians their commercial endeavours had attracted to the tiny island.

Early Twentieth Century Raffles—Raffles Institution to left, Beach Road, reclamation ground and sea to right.
By courtesy of the Library of the Royal Commonwealth Society

The colony's founder, Sir Stamford Raffles of the euphemistically named "Honourable" East India Company, who was then Lieutenant Governor of Bencoolen in Sumatra, Indonesia, had contrived to make the purpose of their endeavour seem noble indeed. He said in 1819, soon after planting the flag on the small Malay fishing settlement that was then the island of Singapore:

> "Our object is not territory, but trade, a commercial emporium and a fulcrum, whence we may extend our influence politically as circumstances may hereafter require. By taking this possession, we put a negative to the Dutch claim of exclusion, and, at the same time, revive the drooping confidence of our allies and friends."

But it was a moot point whether free trade or the destruction of Dutch trading superiority was the larger factor in his mind.

Raffles Hotel is a monument to Sir Stamford's open-armed welcome to all men wishing to trade with Singapore, that natural hub of commerce in Southeast Asia, and it was opened about the same time as the unveiling of the famous statue of the colony's founder which gazes across Singapore's bustling harbour from Empress Place. It is fitting that it should bear his name and that to this day it should proudly display his image at its imposing entrance.

Ironically though, this enduring symbol of British colonial life, as many casual observers take the hotel to be, was built not by the British, but by three Armenian brothers, entrepreneurs named Sarkies, who hailed from Julfa in what is now Turkey.

They had a shrewd eye for opportunity, those Sarkies—for Singapore in the 1880s, when they first arrived, was fast becoming a gambling man's bet.

In 1867 the colony had severed the chafing restriction of the umbilical cord that tied it to the East India Company, which had for too long ensured a kind of benign, if neglectful, rule from distant India. "The Transfer"— of Singapore from the East India Company to the Crown, along with Prince of Wales' Island, as Penang was then known, and Malacca, both on the Malayan Peninsula, the three together comprising the then Straits Settlements —gave Singapore the liberty at last to pursue its original *raison d'etre*: free trade.

The Indian Government had, in the days of its suzerainty, failed to protect the seas around the new colony, which teemed with pirates who preyed on coastal vessels. It had even established a convict settlement on Singapore, to which felons from the Indian mainland were transported.

But a settled, civilian population about 140,000-strong was, after the transfer, able to hold the pirates at bay and to get down to business. The foundations for Malaya's huge present-day rubber exports and for Singapore's crucial role as middleman were laid, for "Mad" Henry Nicholas Ridley who was appointed director of the Botanic Gardens in 1888 was to pioneer the planting of Brazilian rubber seedlings in this region.

Just as important, a revolution in shipping was taking place that benefited not only trade but also tourism. In 1867 the record time for a London–Singapore voyage stood at 116 days; but in 1870 the steamer *Shantung* zipped from Glasgow to Singapore in 42 days, stops included. Not only the speed but also the volume of ships calling at the attractively free port had swollen enormously with the opening of the Suez Canal at the end of 1869, linking the Mediterranean with the Red Sea, and thence with the old "spice route" to the Indian Ocean, the Straits of Malacca and Singapore—ships had formerly plied the immensely longer Cape of Good Hope-Sunda Straits (Indonesia) route. By 1870, 500 vessels a year were passing through the Canal.

All this led to an almost feverish expansion of dock facilities. External communications also improved, with the arrival of telegraph links in the 1860s; so did internal transport, with the Singapore Railway Company busily laying new lines linking the town with New Harbour (now Keppel Harbour). In 1880 the *jinrickisha*, or human-drawn rickshaw, was first imported from Japan, via Shanghai.

Swamps and plantations along the line gave way to warehouses. The building of Cavenagh Bridge over the Singapore River obviated the previous need to negotiate it by ferry; a horse-drawn omnibus service ran the harbour route at 15-minute intervals by 1875, but was soon replaced in 1885 by the Singapore

Tramway Company's steam trams (which however went out of business in the leaner 1890s).

The main impression created in the minds of visitors to the island was of the extreme verdancy of the scenery. One traveller, Isabella Bird, in a letter home describing the two-mile drive from the pier to the city, wrote that "a world of wonders opens at every step". She said: "It is intensely tropical; there are mangrove swamps and fringes of cocoa-palms, and banana-groves, date, sago and travellers' palms, tree-ferns, india-rubber, mango, custard-apple, jack-fruit, durian, lime, pomegranate, pineapples and orchids, and all kinds of strangling and parrot-blossomed trailers . . . There is a perpetual battle between man and the jungle . . .".

Even today, most of the almost two million tourists who visit Singapore each year, and especially those who stay at the elegantly nostalgic Raffles Hotel, would probably say that Singapore still creates similar impressions on them, still communicates a certain Oriental romance. Even if a garden-city-conscious planner's government has since uprooted the trees and arranged them in more convenient places, and in more orderly patterns, the travellers' palms in the Raffles' Palm Court are timeless and unchanging.

Some more alarming features of early Singapore are, however, no longer with us. Tigers, for instance.

Joseph Conrad's story 'The End of the Tether', set in the Singapore of the 1880s, notes that even a quite central area was "shunned by natives after business hours" because of tigers "coming at a loping canter . . . to get a Chinese shopkeeper for supper."

The tiger stories seem to have started in the 1830s. The somewhat quaint belief at the time was that the tigers had somehow appeared on the island, probably by swimming over from mainland Johore in Malaya, and were getting nearer to the city. The truth is probably that the abundance of tigers was a measure of Singapore's increasing development, which cleared their natural jungle habitat, depriving them of both cover and natural prey, thus driving them into the open to hunt the only food left to them—Man.

Government intermittently offered rewards for dead tigers, ranging from $50 to $250 a head, but the beasts lingered on for some years. Probably the last one to roam free in the colony, albeit a captive circus tiger, was to be shot under the billiard room at the Raffles Hotel in 1902.

Back home in Britain, people were frankly incredulous of the scare stories. The magazine, *Punch*, observed satirically of one newspaper report in 1855: "If the population of Singapore is really being converted into food for tigers and the inhabitants are departing as regularly as the steamers, it is high time that something should be done to save the remnant of the populace. Considering that the tigers have evidently got the upper hand, we think they show a sort of moderation in taking only two inhabitants per week . . . We suspect that our eastern contemporary either is indulging in a little romance or is agitated by

Mr G. P. Owen—Mrs Dare's second husband, a leading social light, secretary of the Cricket Club, fire chief and renowned Great White Hunter at a time when Singapore was full of tigers. He married Mrs Dare, original owner of the Raffles Hotel building, after Dare's death in 1907.
By courtesy of Ray Tyers

fears that have grown up under the enervating influence of the climate...."

Certainly, as one reclines today in Raffles Hotel gardens sipping a Singapore Sling in the shadow of skyscrapers, the distant hum of demolition, construction and reclamation work, busy traffic and busy people in one's ears, the idea of Singapore as once a virgin jungle haunted by tigers seems the purest of fantasy.

Even in the 1880s, Singapore was a strange mixture of what Norman Sherry, the Conrad expert, has called "sophistication and primitiveness". The population was certainly small. In 1881, for instance, there were 2,679 Europeans—and 80 Armenians—out of a total population of 139,208.

There were two worlds then. The more glamorous, the exotic, was that of buccaneers full of wild dreams and fantastic plans that Conrad described in *Lord Jim*. The other was the monotonous and—particularly to the womenfolk—frustratingly circumscribed world of the expatriate. The young fortune-seekers, the rogues and plain seadogs who descended on the new Eldorado that was Southeast Asia must all have got their first glimpse of Singapore harbour and the men of the East from the belly of a sampan rowed out from their oceangoing clippers and steamers, much as young Marlow did in the same author's *Youth*:

"The whole length of the jetty was full of people. I saw brown, bronze, yellow faces, the black eyes, the glitter, the colour of an Eastern crowd."

And once lounging on the verandahs of the Sailors' Home, or the latest "in" tiffin room (tiffin being an Anglo-Indian word still used by "old hands" in Singapore for a local lunch, usually curry. Raffles Hotel still boasts a Tiffin Room), these men would, like Conrad's Jim, look on the scene that still awaits the visitor today. Just a stone's throw from the Raffles simmers the world's third busiest port, a "confusion of high sterns, spars, masts and lowered sails."

The early tiffin room scene was one of great joviality and bonhomie among the motley crowd of customers who sought diversion there, and conversation is said to have been of a rollicking nature as captain-owners of the pioneer trading vessels swapped yarns with each other and sought to impress the locals with accounts of their adventures. These tiffin-room tales were almost certainly the source of some of the yarns spun by Conrad into his novels.

Riotous young men, adventurers and sharpsters made the hotel trade a chancy business. The local press of the time contains many outraged comments on miscreants who tried to pass chits instead of money to pay their hotel bills, and on others who skipped before the bill was ever presented.

In 1886 H. W. Lucy, the editor at that time of the London *Daily News*, wrote in his book *West by East* of an unnamed hotel in Singapore where, he said, a placard was prominently displayed in the office stating: "Passengers and boarders are respectfully requested not to ask the manager for any money, as he has strict injunctions not to give same." This, the author said, was not an isolated hint of a certain aspect of social life in those parts. "Even more common is the edict that the servants of the hotel have instructions to hold on to all baggage until bills are paid," he affirmed.

Meanwhile, in the other, more bourgeois world, the pursuit of mammon proceeded in a social climate of genteel boredom, loneliness, languor and intellectual stagnation. The event of each week was the arrival, and departure, of the mail boat. The women tried hard to create a round of gaiety by arranging dances, concerts, theatricals and card parties, but the mainstay of existence for most of them was the dream of one day going "home".

It was boring, oh so boring. Indeed, so stumped were the young bachelors for amusement in their bed-and-breakfast rooms or "messes" (flats shared by several young men) that they plumbed the depths of inanity with deplorable "British public-school" antics, such as pelting coolies working in the boats and on the sea wall, or the staff of a waterside godown (warehouse) with rotten eggs and mangosteen skins that spread deep scarlet stains. The source of a missile was not obvious, so a free fight among the victims frequently ensued, much to the delight of the persecutors.

Meanwhile, the hard workers were probably anxiously scanning the horizon through a telescope for early sight of the next ship, which would mean either business or more mail, this being the surest, if still primitive, method of gaining commercial intelligence at the time.

The art of conversation was in a state as parlous as the community's adolescent sense of humour. In an inward-looking society it was inevitable that small talk, especially in the absence of any stirring local events such as the arrival of a celebrity from the outside world, an important local business deal, or a grand reception by a prominent worthy, should revolve around the trivia of other people's domestic circumstances and prospects in their employment. There are, of course, cynics who maintain that nothing has changed and that it is still possible to hear very similar exchanges among Singapore-based expatriates even today.

It was a society that clung to an etiquette imported from a faraway land. The women insisted on wearing high-necked blouses, flowing skirts, petticoats and even long kid gloves—in a temperature that, as now, never dipped much below 80 degrees Fahrenheit. In fact Edwin Brown, a local impresario at the turn of the century, had an extremely difficult job to break the habit of rehearsing for amateur dramatics in full evening dress. When, to quote his own words, he told his cast that "old clothes" would be rehearsal gear in future, "one lady in the chorus refused to believe that I really dare to be so iconoclastic and came to the next rehearsal in evening dress—a nice black lace one, I remember."

With household electricity still a much debated novelty, these overdressed ladies were kept cool only by the ministrations of the *punkah wallah*, a "native" who sat out on the verandah tugging rhythmically at a long string, attached to his fingers or his toes, to activate the gently draught-inducing sweep of a rattan punkah, or fan.

European men then wore the white duck *baju tutup*, a button-up, high-collared

Cartoon by Dennis Santry, from *Straits Produce*, April 1 1924. This suggests the European-colonial stereotype of the dumb Malay chauffeur (Syce) who is so "simple" that he can imagine "Raffles" might mean somewhere other than the hotel. "Raffles Apa?" means "Raffles what?".
By courtesy of the Library of the Royal Commonwealth Society

tropical white suit, with white canvas boots to match, and rarely went bareheaded in the sun, preferring to shelter beneath a solar topee.

As juniors in the office, they would graduate from travelling to work in a "rickshaw" pulled by a Chinese coolie, to their own horse-drawn buggy, almost inevitably bought from "Daddy" Abrams, whose resourcefulness as a horse and carriage and riding equipment supplier, or indeed of almost anything saleable, was legend (as was his tolerance for bad debts). They would be "complete with fly whisk and all," accountant J. S. M. Rennie tells us, "and a nice smart *sais* standing on a dashboard at the rear." (You will still hear long-term residents in Singapore refer to their "syce", meaning the chaffeur of their sleek Mercedes.)

This was a community so imbued with the spirit of Empire that, when Queen Victoria died in 1901, Edwin Brown could write:

"It was as if the heart of the great British Empire had stopped beating.

Something had happened that seemed to be beyond the power of human intelligence to grasp . . . (Singapore) seemed like a city struck with plague." And yet it was also a society—very different from that of today—in which nobody would have dreamed of speaking to his local servant in English. Malay was the lingua franca for Europeans, Chinese, Malays and Indians alike. This was a rule strictly enforced in mess, club and office. Nonetheless, a Chinese coolie would always unwind his *towchang* (pigtail) from the top of his head, where it was piled up like a woman's bun, as a mark of respect when he entered a European's office.

When a young man first arrived in Singapore it was customary for him to be taken round visiting other offices and then to tour the ladies' boxes. This was far from what it sounds like, an invitation to visit the red light district. The *Buku Merah* (Red Book), a name by which to this day locals insist on calling the *Straits Times Directory of Singapore*, a handbook of local companies, in those days featured a "Ladies Directory" which listed the addresses of European dwellings. Into the letter box outside each of these houses the young hopeful would drop his calling card and the gentlemen's wives would duly enter him on their social roster. Before long, he would receive a summons to dinner—the signal that he had been accepted into the bosom of this almost incestuous microcosm.

There was a preponderance of the male sex and consequently keen competition for female companionship. The dances held once a month at the Tanglin Club were very popular among the young men, who kept the telephone lines busy for days ahead of the event, trying to secure partners.

Another place to meet the ladies in the evening was on the Esplanade, then almost synonymous with today's Padang—the green sward in front of City Hall—for until massive reclamation works in 1889 the Padang was half its present size and fronted straight on to the sea.

In the cooler evenings at about 5.00 pm (dusk falls with almost monotonous regularity from about 6.30 pm in Singapore, reaching pitch darkness by 7 pm), the pallid lady wives and daughters would as one emerge from their homes in the European quarter to perform an extraordinary social ritual. This was the evening "turn" in horse-drawn carriages around the Esplanade and along the waterfront. Gigs, victorias, gharries, buggies and barouches paraded for two hours in a double row, crossing and re-crossing each others' paths.

Apart from cricket on the Padang, yachting and a modest variety of other sports, there was little in the way of recreation for the colony's inhabitants. Drinking *stengahs* (half-glass measures of whisky) and scandal-mongering, possibly even at the aptly named "Scandal Point", were therefore popular pastimes.

One of the chief amusements, however, was—very home-made—amateur dramatics. According to Edwin Brown, even by 1901 these were pretty rough at the edges, and we are indebted to the same witness for the information that the custom of free drinks to all performers had a good deal to do with the lack of profit when the balance-sheet came to be drawn up. As he pointed out, "it did not matter much if the company was an hour or so late in starting—it was much easier to amuse people in the old days . . ."

At one musical rehearsal the infuriated conductor said, "Ladies, you can't sing and you're not a bit of good in the choir. You might get up on these (pointing to the gas-brackets hanging from the roof), and give a horizontal bar display; you would be quite as good at it as at singing and the men would be much more amused!" At which, the ladies walked out in a huff.

The local theatre scene was marred by petty personal jealousies among would-be stars, for this was a tiny, introverted community. The audiences were just as irritable and the newspapers regularly printed complaints from people who, in the absence of properly organised booking arrangements, had failed to obtain their seats, others having taken them.

The unfortunate tone set at some of the first performances on record, in 1833, continued much the same over the years. One pioneer effort, according to the *Singapore Chronicle* "afforded more abundance of amusement to some, both off and on the stage . . . but the whole would have gone off much better had several of them kept sober, and others remembered their parts better."

One of the more curious theatrical conventions of the day was that men played the female parts, it being considered grossly immodest for real women to play them. One local Church of England clergyman in 1844 preached from the pulpit a tirade against the theatre and actors in general, especially women playing parts like Shakespeare's Portia in *The Merchant of Venice*—as a result of which, however, he was severely taken to task by the local press, since he was referring indirectly to an established visiting professional actress, and the local theatres played to noticeably fuller houses for weeks thereafter.

Among the local "female impersonators" were the brothers George and Julius Dare, sons of Captain George Julius Dare, a seagoing China trader whose family home, which was also a tiffin house, was at the corner of Beach and Bras Basah roads. This house was on the present site of the Raffles Hotel and was probably bought from the Dare family by the Armenian Sarkies brothers in 1886.

The Beach Road area had ceased to be fashionable as a European residential area by the time the Sarkies arrived. But the land was not going cheap and perhaps George Mildmay Dare, a mere company clerk—his father's business had been ruined by his supposed right hand man, in 1855, just before the 50-year-old captain's death—found the Sarkies' offer for the family house quite a windfall.

The shoreline in the early days of Raffles Hotel was right at the edge of the then aptly named Beach Road, which offered a clear view of the harbour and the seas beyond. At high tide, the water would lap right up to the front doorsteps of the houses, and of the hotel.

We know little about the Dares' house or why it attracted the Sarkies' attention when they were scouting around for a property to convert into a hotel. But it seems the place had already built up a sizeable reputation as a tiffin room, and, as we have seen, tiffin rooms were lively meeting places in those days.

Clearly, the Sarkies were no risk-takers nor innovators—they were not bold enough to create a market but moved into Singapore when there was already a healthy market, as was obvious from the proliferation of hotels, tiffin rooms and rendezvous which had sprung up, together with many small boarding houses and pensions *en famille* for young bachelors.

Equally, however, they clearly were not afraid of competition, for here was plenty of it. Much of the hotel action seems to have been concentrated in the old city centre, around the Esplanade, High Street and Coleman Street, however.

Why the Sarkies picked Beach Road is not certain. Perhaps it was a more peaceful and gracious, if fading, area, with a fine harbour view and the added advantage of declining rivals leaving their clientele ripe for the picking. The hotels they built in South-east Asia—the Raffles in Singapore, Eastern and Oriental in Penang, and Strand in Rangoon—are all living testimony that the Sarkies had a sense of elegance and dignity, and they probably scorned in a supercilious way to get mixed up with the hoi polloi, the rowdies, the sailors, the young bachelors, the commercial travellers and the P & O crowds that haunted the tiffin rooms, Tingle Tangle Club and the like amid the general hubbub that was and still is Singapore's city centre.

They certainly foresaw the great potential of Singapore as a tourist centre, though not, perhaps, with quite the same degree of prescience as J. S. M. Rennie, who, watching the ubiquitous public works in the city in the 1930s, remarked: "One is forced to opine that Singapore's main business will become that of a health resort and place of visit for American and Australian trippers." Today, tourism earns Singapore more than one billion Singapore dollars a year. The Raffles is one of the warm human factors behind those cold statistics.

2 THE FOUNDERS

The Sarkies brothers, founders of the Raffles, were, as we have noted, Armenians and in Armenia's troubled history lies the reason for their family's and countrymen's wanderings all over the globe, so that till today, tenacious little minority communities still cling to an ancient Armenian culture in India, Australia, Europe and certain cities of the United States.

Singapore and Indonesia, with the passage of history, proved to be but transit points for the peripatetic Armenians, as they departed in a steady stream from the Indian subcontinent—where most of the older generation, and probably the Sarkies too, received their education—to Australia or America. Nonetheless, in both countries the Armenians have left their mark, visible in the shape of churches and hotels like the Raffles.

First public mention of the proposed establishment of Raffles Hotel was on 19 September 1887, when the *Singapore Free Press* noted: "Mr Sarkies from Penang is said to have taken the building at present occupied as the Raffles boarding establishment which he proposes to convert into a hotel at early date".

The Sarkies had already been established as hoteliers in Penang since about 1884, and of the four founding brothers—Martin, Tigran, Aviet and Arshak—the eldest, Martin, had been working in Penang as an engineer since the end of 1869.

It was when Tigran left his trading business in Java to join Martin in Penang that the hotel enterprise really got underway. The two opened the Eastern Hotel there in 1884, and, the following year, the Oriental in the same town. The two names were later to be combined into the Eastern and Oriental, or "E and O" as it became affectionately known to a large clientele in the period when Arshak, the youngest brother, was the driving force there.

Aviet joined the partnership in 1884. He seems also to have been something of an engineer and architect and to have left his personal mark on the architectural design of the Sarkies hotels.

Arshak, who was by the 1920s a half-owner in all the Sarkies enterprises, including the Raffles, had joined the family firm in 1891, shortly after the eldest, Martin, had retired.

Successful and astute businessmen that they were, it was hardly likely that the Sarkies would long ignore the commercial and economic ferment in Singapore. Their attention may perhaps have been attracted in 1887 by reports of the feverish activity surrounding Queen Victoria's Golden Jubilee celebrations there, and the unveiling on that occasion of Sir Stamford Raffles's statue now standing in Empress Place.

The period has been called the "high noon of Empire": optimism, confidence and expansion were the order of the day.

But press reports at that time ascribe a different motivation to the Sarkies' removal to Singapore—the brothers were disgruntled with an increase in the rent of their E and O property and were actually considering abandoning the Penang operations altogether in favour of starting a hotel in Singapore. As it turned out, they did not leave Penang, but widened their horizons.

According to the *Penang Gazette*, the E and O rent was raised from $200 to $350 a month—"a joke which Mr Sarkies does not appear to appreciate, and he has consequently decided to seek new, and let us hope happier, hunting grounds".

As a result of what the Sarkies considered to be a rapacious move on the part of their landlord, they acquired the Raffles Girls' Boarding School (which seems to have superceded the old Dares' tiffin room) in Singapore, which they planned to extend and convert into a first class hotel. The *Penang Gazette* waxed almost rhapsodical over the project, declaring: "When we say that the hotel will contain 48 bedrooms—each with its own private verandah and bathroom—some idea of the lines upon which the building will be constructed may easily be imagined.

"A large and commodious billiard room capable of containing four tables is to be provided and new furniture has been ordered from Europe and Sourabaya. The Raffles Hotel, for such is to be the name, is expected to be completed in March and we trust that the enterprise will in every way prove fruitful."

In hotels of the time, it was quite unthinkable not to have a billiard room,

RAFFLES HOTEL.

2, BEACH ROAD, SINGAPORE.

Messrs. SARKIES BROTHERS have the honour to inform their friends and patrons that they will open the above Hotel on the 1st of December next.

The situation is one of the best and healthiest in the town, facing the sea, and within a few minutes' walk of the Public Offices and the Square.

Great care and attention for the comfort of Boarders and Visitors have been taken in every detail, and those frequenting it will find every convenience and home comfort.

From the great experience Messrs. SARKIES BROTHERS have gained in the management of the Eastern and the Oriental Hotels in Penang, and the success that has attended them, they are confident that the "RAFFLES HOTEL" will meet a great want long felt in Singapore. The sole endeavour of the proprietors will be to attend to the comfort of their Visitors.

Rooms can now be engaged.

TERMS MODERATE.

SARKIES BROTHERS,
Proprietors.

Nov. 19.

SARKIES BROTHERS beg to intimate that they are prepared to undertake catering for Breakfasts, Tiffins, Dinners, and Suppers, for Public Balls and Entertainments.

Advertisement from the *Singapore Free Press*, November 1887.
By courtesy of *Straits Times*, Singapore

hence the special mention of this facility—it would be like not offering a swimming pool nowadays.

Notwithstanding the favourable reception given by the local press to the new hotel, it seems to have been overshadowed in its early years by the larger and older Hotel de l'Europe, although the occasional advertisement during the late 1880s testifies to the fact that it remained healthily in business. It does not seem really to have come into prominence until about 1899, when substantial renovation, extension and the advent of electric lighting again brought it to the public's attention.

The Raffles however was by no means the only enterprise, even in Singapore, for the empire-building Sarkies. They ran, for a number of years, tiffin rooms they had acquired in Raffles Square (now the famous Raffles Place), which they eventually sold to a Chinese purchaser; and in 1923 they bought the Sea View at Katong, which was demolished in the 1960s.

Raffles Hotel.

PATRONIZED by Royalty, Nobility and Distnguished Personages, including

H. R. H. Prince Damron
H. R. H. Prince Sevaster.
His Grace The Duke of Newcastle.
The Right Hon'ble The Earl of Dysart.
Lord and Lady Braye.
Lord Dormer.
Lord Cecil
Lord Valletort.
Major General Sir Henry Collett, K.C.B.
Sir Francis Boileau, Bar:
Sir John James William Henry Spencer.
Sir Edmond Hill
Brigadier-General Gossit C. B
Baron Hamern.
Baron Bu. slar.
Baron Wendelstadt.
Sir Somers Vine.
Count Getelle.
Count Spee.
The late Sir Elliot Boville, Justice, S S.
The Hon'ble Lionel Cox, Chief Justice, S.S.
Major-General Sir Charles Warren, G.C.M.G., K.C.B., R.E.
Major-General Molyneux.
His Excellency Major-General Jones Vaughan, Commanding the Troops, S.S.
H.M. Officers of Army and Navy.

This First Class Hotel which has just been elnarged by 30 additional suites, is facing and commanding an extensive view of the Harbour, close to the Public Offices, Mercantile Quarters and the Esplanade.

Suites consisting of Sitting-Room, Bed-Rooms, Dressing-Room with private bath room attached.

No expense has been spared by us to meet the requirements and demands of the Public and is very comfort is guaranteed.

There is a Ladies Waiting and Dressing Room fitted with all requisites.

SARKIES BROTHERS—Proprietors.

Dec. 11.

Advertisement from the *Singapore Free Press* of December 20, 1898, and through the 1890s. Many of the "VIP" names so proudly quoted seem almost to have faded into obscurity now.

By courtesy of *Straits Times*

In 1910 the Raffles Hotel, short of space while the Palm Court wings were being built, took over the top two floors of Oranje Building in Stamford Road, now Stamford House, as an annexe, until the building became the Orange Hotel under different management in 1933. Last of the brothers' ventures, however, was the Strand Hotel in Rangoon, which eventually became Aviet Sarkies' special responsibility.

By 1923 a travellers' handbook to the "seaports of the Far East" was able to assure its readers that "no hotel keepers in the East are more famous than Messrs Sarkies Brothers, pioneers in their line of business in the towns where they have established themselves so well". This assertion is borne out by a joke current in Singapore and Malaysia at the time, which went thus: "Who are the Orang Sakai?" (the Orang Sakai are aboriginals indigenous to Malaya.) Answer: "A race of hotel proprietors inhabiting the jungles of Penang and Singapore."

The personalities of Martin, Tigran and Aviet do not emerge from the available records very clearly—that they were industrious and shrewd businessmen, as well as lovers of old world elegance, is clear from their hotel ventures and the buildings they erected. They were probably rather dignified and serious men. But the odd man out seems to have been Arshak, the youngest.

The family business ended with a whimper and bankruptcy in 1931, soon after Arshak's death. Tigran had retired in 1917, and Aviet had died in 1923. The company's failure was in part attributable to Arshak's over-generous nature, although there was of course also a worldwide slump at the time.

Arshak is the one of whom we have the most detailed portrait, clearly because his warm, open-hearted disposition and hospitality were legendary in the East. He seems to have been an energiser too—it may not be a coincidence that much of the brothers' expansion took place after Arshak's joining the company in 1891. But his methods were not good business, he loved gambling on the horses, and his lavish extensions to his special pride and joy, the E and O, at just the wrong time, proved his undoing.

Despite his ebullient nature Arshak apparently died a sick and bitter man, uncharacteristically reclusive in his declining years. He quarrelled frequently with his partners, by then another Armenian family, the Arathoons, and left the company in complete disarray at his death.

There are a number of witnesses to the brothers' charitable nature. They are known to have helped numerous travellers, not all of whom were fellow Armenians, who found themselves stranded in a strange country. One writer in the 1930s described the hotels as "monuments to their kindly memory".

Arshak continued this trait of kindness to a fault. It has been said that he ran the E and O so as to be able to entertain his friends rather than with any idea of showing a healthy balance sheet. He was a secret benefactor, too, for it became known only after his death that when hard times hit Malaya in the rubber slump of the 1920s and unemployment became rife, he drew selflessly on his own resources in order to assist the unfortunate.

Arshak was married, with three daughters. One old staff member swears that

Aviet Sarkies. From *Twentieth Century Impressions of British Malaya*.

Tigran Sarkies. From *Twentieth Century Impressions of British Malaya*.

Arshak Sarkies. From *Twentieth Century Impressions of British Malaya*.

he had two 'wives', and that there was insanity in the family. Arshak certainly ran his affairs in a crazy but endearing fashion.

One recipient of his benefactions, Victor Boldy, an Armenian who later became a member of the Armenian community in the Hague, Netherlands, was born at the E and O on January 7, 1903 largely thanks to Arshak's freely offered hospitality. His parents were en route for Surabaya, when they landed in Penang. Spotting Mrs Boldy's advanced pregnancy and recognising the couple as fellow Armenians, the chivalrous Arshak, in the true spirit of Armenian fellowship, immediately offered a room, where Mrs Boldy duly gave birth.

Arshak was not only generous but gregarious by nature—at ease in any company, lowly or exalted, rich or poor.

The character of the man is faithfully portrayed in an account by George Bilainikin, an editor of the *Penang Echo*, of his first encounter with Noel Coward, who was accompanied by Lord Amherst:

> "Arshak, stern, red-faced with Semitic nose, sat as usual before a small *stengah* (literally "half" in Malay, but denoting in many parts of the East a whisky and soda). He looked up and slowly extended his sensitive and critical hand to the visitors. Apparently he liked them. I knew by Arshak's expression whether he approved.
>
> "He spread his freemasonry sparingly but men who were his friends knew a generosity difficult to match. Arshak had a curious pride, a curious impertinence that one may ascribe to his Semitic origin. He never asked visitors whether they had been comfortable or had enjoyed themselves. He told them firmly they had enjoyed themselves, had been comfortable and anticipated, accurately, that they would reply that they had been made happy by his staff. Then, silence.
>
> "Coward and Amherst talked and laughed happily with Arshak. And Arshak was not overwhelmed. He had dined with royalty, millionaire statesmen, diplomatists. He counted among his friends barefooted Tamil liftmen, watchmen, car attendants, drivers, cleaners, water carriers."

The same writer testifies to Arshak's original sense of humour and says he was particularly proud of a feat he performed on festive occasions of waltzing round the ballroom without spilling a drop from the glass of whisky and soda that he balanced on his bald head.

Arshak was a gentle cynic, whose outward worldliness concealed the generous streak to which reference has been made. According to Bilainikin, he looked aggressive and almost angry if friends asked him whether he had ever kept count of the number of men he had helped during periods of rubber and tin depression. He regarded this as a secret between himself and the recipients themselves. But there were dozens of customers whose accounts were "forgotten" on Arshak's instructions. Some of them were formerly rich rubber planters and tin miners who were able to leave Malaya thanks to Arshak's provision of funds for a passage costing between £50 and £60.

Friends recalled that Arshak always handed over a small sum to the unfortunates that they might land in Europe with a few pounds in their pockets.

His last year was a troubled one, with the world depression taking a heavy toll in Malaya. Mercifully his death spared him the sorrow of hearing the bankruptcy court's decision that his widow and daughter, who for 40 years had occupied a corner of a small annexe of the E and O hotel, must leave their home.

But at least his funeral was on a grand scale, attended by all the luminaries of Penang high society. There was a moving address by Mr Justice Sproule, then Resident Councillor of Penang, who was ironically enough to hear the Sarkies Brothers bankruptcy case later that same year, in his capacity as Acting Chief Justice.

The last partner in the Sarkies Brothers' business, Martyrose Sarkies Arathoon, who had quarrelled with Arshak continually over his conduct of the hotel books (Arshak being in the 1920s and 1930s half-owner of all the ventures and therefore a frequent visitor to the Raffles to inspect operations there), was left "holding the baby" when Arshak died. It was Arathoon who took the rap for the bankruptcy proceedings.

The Armenians of Singapore say this is a tale of tragedy common enough in their community, which has a sad record of internal feuding and of sons' failure to fulfil their fathers' hopes.

If the collapse of the Sarkies enterprises was a sad one, particularly after years of brilliant success, the brothers' arrival in Singapore was not exactly greeted with a fanfare. It was a modest start: in 1887, the year of Queen Victoria's Golden Jubilee, the Raffles boasted only 20 rooms in a single block, the Dares' original house, which has been described as an "unpretentious building". There are few references to the hotel during the remaining years of the decade—not even an advertisement, although the scattered mentions that exist indicate a thriving and popular enough establishment.

In these days, when world snooker tournaments are watched by millions of television viewers and huge prizes are offered for a single break in such popular contests as "Pot Black", it is amusing to read that the prize for the handicap which inaugurated the new billiard table at the Raffles was "a handsome gold watch". But the timepiece was a generous gift of the proprietors, who also made entrance to the match free to members of the Singapore Cricket, Sporting, Tanglin, Teutonia and Masonic Clubs.

The travel itch was spreading at this time and the number of genuine tourists was growing. They were not all of the most desirable type, for travel was no longer restricted to the wealthy. The hotel business became slightly more risky, but potentially much more lucrative.

Just before the Sarkies took over it had been reported that hotel proprietors, native tailors and others were being victimised by "some impudent and barefaced strangers—swindlers who engaged rooms in first-class hotels and rode in two-horse carriages". They ran up chits and got credit for large sums. A "new and undesirable class of European inhabitant" was said to have begun to collect in Singapore "having passed by degrees through Egypt (a sink of iniquity for people of a certain class) to Ceylon and on to Singapore by taking a deck passage in some cheap steamer".

But "the upper crust" was not deterred from paying visits to such exotic parts; perhaps the risk of being in close contact with the seamier aspect of life in the magnetic Far East added zest.

One of the earliest glimpses of the new hotel was given by Mrs Florence Caddy, accompanying the Duke of Sutherland on his yacht *Sans Peur* in 1889. She referred to a "Malay luncheon" there and said she and her companions also took time out to "read the papers and find what the world had been doing" and "cooled ourselves in the verandah of the Raffles Hotel."

But an even more illustrious visitor the same year was the writer Rudyard Kipling, who rode into port with his friends Ted and Aleck Hill aboard the *Madura*, which he used as his sleeping quarters for his short visit of about four days, en route for Japan and San Francisco. The shortness of his stay however did not prevent him from pronouncing judgment on the Raffles, in a somewhat pompous manner:

> "Providence conducted me along a beach, in full view of five miles of shipping—five solid miles of masts and funnels—to a place called Raffles Hotel, where the food is excellent as the rooms are bad. Let the traveller take note. Feed at Raffles and sleep at the Hotel de l'Europe."

Somewhat in the manner of theatres who quote only part of the critics' reviews —the good parts—on their billboards, the Sarkies turned the tables on the bard of the British Empire by extracting just the words "where the food is excellent" for use in their advertisements.

Perhaps left-handed compliments such as Kipling's, as well as the increasing superiority of the Europe, goaded the Sarkies into action, or perhaps it was simply the increasing volume of tourist traffic, but in 1890 the hotel's central block was extended in both directions by throwing out two handsome wings, the beginning of the Palm Court enclosure. There may at first have been plans to continue work immediately, but the Sarkies cannot have failed to note the trade depression which set in the following year and the simultaneous fall in the value of silver on which the colony's currency, the Straits dollar, was based.

They pulled in their horns for a while, but not until after a new billiard room with four new tables, imported from London, had been installed. These stood beside a bar made of teak with a marble top and backed by a large plate glass mirror. Even at the opening ceremony, when the room was crowded with visitors, the air was said to be "cool and pleasant". One of the billiard tables, and a Victorian era scoreboard, is still to be seen at the Raffles today.

After five years had passed the economic climate had revived sufficiently to permit another enlargement which added another section of Beach Road land

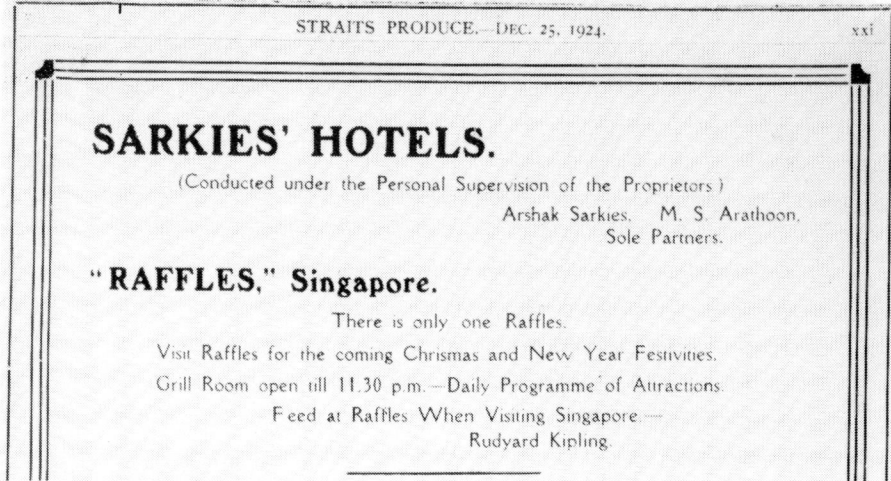

Advertisement from *Straits Produce*, 25 December 1924.
By courtesy of the Library of the Royal Commonwealth Society

and 20 new bedrooms to the hotel, a section previously occupied by the American consulate.

A further spur to speedy action must have been the existence of two small hotels right next door to the Raffles, which made the competition hot. These hotels, the Beach and the Victoria, were on a site which was advocated as being suitable for a mooted new town hall.

Another prospective site was the vacant seafront land facing the Raffles. Although it was suggested that the only persons who could reasonably object would be the Sarkies, they, it was stated, so far from raising any objection, would actually like the new town hall to be erected between their hotel and the sea.

If they did indeed say this, it seems odd, unless it be that they anticipated additional custom for their hotel spilling over from functions and the general to-ing and fro-ing at the proposed municipal centre opposite. Or perhaps, as newcomers to a tight little community, they did not want to be called dogs in the manger at this early stage.

The expectation of further development of their Beach Road area and a resulting increase in custom as well as large-scale renovations at the Hotel de l'Europe may have been reasons prompting their decision in 1897 to embark on a really massive renovation, a move which was to catapult the Raffles from little more than a humble lodging house to a fine hotel described in passing by *The Sphere* of London in 1905 as "The Savoy of Singapore". But the main reason for the costly gamble was the rapid growth of Singapore, by then the seventh busiest port in the world.

The work began in July 1897 and finished in November 1899, taking five months longer than had been planned. But it was a big and ambitious job.

The alterations entailed demolition of the existing centre block, and the erection in its place of a three-storey block with a much larger superficial area. A Renaissance style of architecture was adopted.

A wide, richly decorated verandah ran round all four sides of the building, sheltering the rooms from sun and rain. The frontal approach led to a T-shaped dining hall of great grandeur: its 96 ft by 67 ft floor, with 36 ft wings, was paved in Carrara marble, and galleries supported by ornate columns and arches looked down on the centre portion from both of the two storeys above, the whole being crowned by an elaborately ornamented skylight and ventilator that filtered sun and air to the interior. Access to the verandahs was provided by massive carved doors, while at the far end the main staircase, of wood construction with fine mouldings and flanked by bronze statues set on plinths formed by the stair newels, swept majestically to the upper floors. Two private dining rooms, decorated on the same lines as the main hall, were set one on each side of the staircase. The ground floor, which boasted an entrance porch at each corner, housed a reception lobby and the hotel office as well as bedrooms with dressing and bathrooms attached. Similar residential accommodation was provided on the first and second floors, and two of the rooms on the first were set apart for Tigran Sarkies, who was responsible for the day-to-day running of the hotel.

Small wonder that such sybaritic luxury should have led to a claim by the proprietors that they were providing facilities that made the Raffles "equal to any hotel in the East".

Of particular pride to the owners was the "double electric light installation", each dynamo of which was said to be capable of lighting "800 16-candle incandescent lights, in addition to five arc lights of 2000 candles each". The arc lights illuminated the entrance from the road and the stables and outbuildings. Electric fans cooled the dining hall and private dining rooms, and were available on request in all bedrooms. The entire hotel was lighted by electricity.

The installation was an innovation which established the Sarkies as go-ahead, forward-looking businessmen. So it is strange to discover that it was strenuously resisted in some quarters. But the advent of electricity was still a topic of some controversy in the Singapore of 1899, with a surprisingly strong lobby against it.

A gossip writer, who anonymously ran a column "On the Verandah" in the *Straits Times*, summarised the reactionary feelings of the lobby when he proclaimed: "I am not sure that I want electric light anywhere, save in a ship's cabin and in thronged thoroughfares . . . Electric light is still the toy of civilisation. What do we want with toys? Did we sail through the gate of Suez bent on pleasure? Did we come to Asia to spend our time in clamouring for a miserable mimicry of metropolitan luxury?"

Some Singaporeans will tell you that the immigrant pioneer's disgust at the intrusion of Western "decadence" is still heard in local pronouncements on the adoption of new "fads".

Press Advertisement of 1905.
By courtesy Roberto Pregarz, Raffles Hotel

THE FOUNDERS 33

As far as ventilation was concerned, a compromise was adopted by the reconstructed Raffles. Although electric fans were installed, the punkah wallahs were allowed to stay on as a complementary luxury and they were a familiar sight right into the 1920s. They sat in the public rooms and verandahs with a toe attached to a cord fixed to a white sheet of cloth suspended from the ceiling. A regular up and down motion of the foot kept the sheet moving to create a draught of air and the wallahs were said to be able to maintain the rhythm even when the monotony of their task caused them to fall asleep.

Completion of the new block meant that the hotel now boasted 100 rooms. And, perhaps most important, a French chef was engaged.

In the true tradition of the sneaky journalist, a *Straits Times* man crept back incognito after the opening, to see for himself the everyday workings of the new hotel. He accorded it praise in general but, as any good journalist is wont, had to find fault somewhere. This one was apparently of a somewhat lecherous turn of mind for he wrote that alas for "flirtation facilities", the four Raffles Hotel

Evening Drinks at the Raffles.
From *Present Day Impressions of the Far East and Prominent and Progressive Chinese at Home and Abroad*, edited by W. Feldwick, 1917

drawing rooms were "exposed to the glance of everyone who moves along the passage. There is not a single screen behind which to seek shelter from the raking fire of curious eyes. Mr Sarkies must get a lady to advise him better."

By 1908 the Raffles could be described in the words of one report as "a building of noble proportions and imposing appearance", covering 200,000 square feet and commanding" an unrivalled panoramic view of the harbour and the adjacent islands, and conveniently situated within easy reach of the chief business centres". According to this account, the rooms by then numbered 150—"rooms" in those days automatically meant suites, complete with sitting room, bedroom, and dressing room, with attached bathroom. The popularity of the hotel was evidenced by the fact that all the rooms were almost always occupied, it was stated.

About the same time, advertisements proclaimed that the hotel boasted its own livery stables, and laundry, as well as "rubber-tyred jinrickshaws", bicycle and motor-stands, even a darkroom for amateur photographers and sample storage room for commercial travellers. Hotel runners were available to board all incoming and outgoing steamers, to assist passengers with luggage, and no doubt, tout for custom.

Meanwhile, the Sarkies had taken on another partner, a fellow Armenian called Thaddeus Paul. Tigran Sarkies had died by 1917, in Vienna. Another Armenian couple, the Stephens, figured on lease agreements in the 1920s.

Another trade slump in 1909–11, and the First World War, 1914–18, perhaps brought a further hiatus in the hotel's physical development, but an account in 1917 by W. Feldwick reveals a very organised establishment indeed. The author said that Raffles was the only hotel in the Straits Settlements that had on its premises its own government post office and telegraph office, its own refreshment room, a bakery from which, beside the hotel supplies, bread was delivered to outside customers, an internal ice and cold-storage plant and its own slaughter house—away from the hotel—at which animals were killed and then sent to cold storage in the hotel refrigerators. It was also the only hotel in which every room had a direct telephone.

Feldwick reported that further improvements were to be made during the next two years. Forty more bedrooms were to be added and plans were ready for new sanitation on the flushing system, while all the bathroom walls were to be tiled. These improvements, he said, would have been effected earlier but for the war. In 1918 the rooms totalled 200.

When cars became all the rage, it was a healthy development for the still young but booming rubber trade. And never tardy in matters of fashion, the Raffles naturally had a motor garage by 1917, described by Feldwick as "modern and complete", containing 13 cars of British and French make, and three motor lorries for luggage and goods.

Not that the rickshaw-man had died out. Far from it—even as late as 1928, the tourist and writer Horace Bleackley was complaining of the rickshaw-wallah's obtuseness, saying that he was "the most thick-headed Chinaman that ever

BY MOTOR FROM SHIP TO HOTEL

By courtesy of the Library of the Royal Commonwealth Society

breathed" and that if he was told to take a fare to the Europe Hotel, he was quite likely to take him to the Raffles.

Perhaps the Raffles management had been sharp enough to bribe the rickshaw-men to do just that? How else was the hotel to compete against the irritatingly superior Europe?

But the rickshaw-men still found the Raffles Hotel pitch lucrative: in late 1923 some 400 of them fought, not far from the hotel, around the Rochore Canal Road area, "with spears, knives, poles, roofing, timbers, sticks and stones", according to one account, to decide which of the two rival groups, the Hengwha or the Hockcha, should have the right to occupy the pitch outside the hotel.

The police were obliged to charge with fixed bayonets (some accounts also say they fired into the air); one coolie was killed, several taken to hospital and about 60 arrested, of whom about 23 were imprisoned for one month and bound over to keep the peace for three months, and the others fined.

The fighting continued for a whole day and was serious enough to keep the shops in the area closed for a week.

But apart from such diversions, life was generally getting very comfortable in Singapore. The jungle had been tamed. The last tiger story seems to have been the one already enshrined in Raffles Hotel mythology and therefore obligatory to retell, although the tiger in question was a rather sad escaped circus specimen.

It happened in August 1902, according to the fullest account, given in Edwin A. Brown's *Indiscreet Memories*. This was to the effect that the tiger was shot under the billiard room of the hotel. After escaping from a show in Beach Road, the beast had been free for some time when, late at night, it gave the fright of his life to the boy in charge of the billiard room by peering at him through the low railing of the verandah. After hiding for a while the boy crept to the doorway and fled as fast as he could.

Early next morning, the tiger was located under the room, which, in the manner common in Malaya, stood on stilts raised about four feet from the ground. The headmaster of Raffles School (now Raffles Institution), Mr Charlie Phillips, Singapore's crack rifle shot, was immediately summoned, being woken from his sleep after a very late night at the ball at Government House. Charlie, in none too good a mood—his head was throbbing as a result of the excesses of the night before—at first gave the messenger a rough time, but having eventually grasped the urgency of the situation, took his Enfield rifle and some cartridges and, clad only in his pyjamas, rushed to the scene of the drama.

Stretching himself at full length, Charlie peered into the gloom under the billiard room but could not discern the animal's presence. Suddenly he thought he saw the creature and fired three rapid shots. Unhappily he was mistaken, possibly because of the effects of the Government House whisky, for he found that his target had been one of the brick supports of the building. Probably the

The Raffles in the 1920s.
By courtesy of Mr Roberto Pregarz, who was given it by an Australian guest

tiger was by now more scared than any of the onlookers for it lay doggo, and for a long time nothing could be seen. At last, however, the headmaster saw its eyes gleaming in the dark, and that was sufficient. A well directed shot took it between those gleaming eyes and the unfortunate beast's circus career was summarily terminated.

Charlie accepted the congratulations showered upon him none too graciously. Not only had his sleep been disturbed but his perfectly good pair of pyjamas had been ruined too!

The incident, of course, gained in the telling, and quickly all sorts of hair raising stories were in circulation. Many people came to believe that the tiger had created havoc in the billiard room itself. One version even had the enraged animal leaping on to the billiard table and dying on the green baize. But old hands testified to the veracity of the version given by Edwin Brown.

3 THE DANCING YEARS

A significant social change was effected by the arrival in the 1920s and 1930s of more and more European women, usually wives, a factor which unfortunately also rendered the social atmosphere much stiffer, as the "memsahibs" strove to inject propriety and "Class" into the formerly rumbustious adventurers' playground that pioneer Singapore had been.

The memoirs of several contemporary writers remarked on this, but the most trenchant comment came from journalist Ian Morrison in his *Malayan Postscipt* of 1942, in which he advanced a private theory that the arrival of white women in the tropics had an adverse effect upon the men and that in the old days, when officials and planters had their native mistresses, they were closer to the indigenous people.

"The white woman has inevitably tried to recreate England, and usually Surbiton, in the tropics. All these things, in my opinion, have tended to soften the white man and cut him off from the life and people of the country," he averred.

In contrast to the wild, exotic world that greeted Conrad, the scene in Singapore in 1936 was epitomised by the words of Bruce Lockhart, a former rubber estate manager turned journalist and intelligence agent. "Raffles appeared to me to be more decorous and more middle-class than any Bournemouth hotel on a Sunday."

With the better supply of womenfolk, however, dancing became attractive as an evening pastime. By the 1920s, there were dances about three times a week at the Raffles, very much the haunt of the young folk in those days, while their stuffier bosses frequented the "up-market" Hotel de l'Europe. The two hotels' weekly dance programmes combined meant you could if you wished dance on six nights a week in Singapore.

Full evening dress including tail coats was the order of the day, although white jackets were also permitted as a concession to the heat. Many young bachelors, revolting against a mode of dress that was highly unsuitable to dancing in the tropics, opted for the cooler and briefer mess jacket irreverently known as the "bum freezer", and established by sheer *force majeure* their right to defy what today would be regarded as an absurd convention.

But if you went on the floor "improperly" dressed, the orchestra at the Raffles would stop playing and you would be asked to leave the floor. Or, in another system, if the managers were concerned that you should not "lose face" so publicly, a diminutive "buttons" would slip on to the floor and discreetly press a card into your hand requesting you to leave. These practices continued right up to the Second World War.

The Singapore population was predominantly young and the youth of both sexes resolutely refused to be deterred by tropical temperatures or arbitrary

Cartoon from *Straits Produce*, October 2, 1922. This shows how Raffles Hotel had become the in-place for the young set to meet.
By courtesy of the Library of the Royal Commonwealth Society

E & O.

OPENING OF BALL ROOM.

We have previously had occasion to refer to the latest enterprise of Messrs. Sarkies Bros. in providing a splendid adjunct to the E. & O. in the shape of a new ball room with a floor space of 77 feet long by 57 feet broad. The full description given in our Xmas supplement makes it superfluous to repeat the details of the building then given. New Year's night was selected by Mr. Arshak Sarkies as an appropriate date for the official opening and for the performance of this ceremony he was fortunate to secure the kind services of the wife of the Hon'ble Resident Councillor, Mrs. Voules. There was a remarkable response on the part of the public to the request for early booking of tables and it speaks volumes for the management that over 450 guests were accommodated with seats. A couple of hundred visitors who had dined elsewhere augmented the merry throng after dinner for which the menu was as follows:—

1 Hors d'oeuvres, 2 Julienne Soup, 3 Fillet of Siangin, Tartare Sauce, 4 Grilled Lamb Chop, 5 Pigeon and Pate de foie gras en aspic, 6 Roast Turkey, Truffled and Ham-Cranberry Sauce, 7 Iced Asparagus, Vinegar Sauce, 8 Trifle, 9 Coupe St. Jacque, 10 Dessert, 11 Coffee. There was a big gathering at the new ballroom at 10-15.

Sir Arthur Adams, standing upon a chair, said he rose for the purpose of introducing somebody, he believed, with whom they were already well acquainted who once again came before them as a benefactor of local humanity—Mr. Arshak Sarkies (loud applause)—one of the tribe of the Orang Sarkais (laughter). As a hotel proprietor who could beat him? (Hear Hear). They were all indebted to him. Those who had lived in Penang for all, half or quarter of the time that had been the speaker's happy lot here knew that Mr. Sarkies had done more than anybody else to make that time a pleasant one for all. He was no absolute altruist any more than any of them. He was out to make money just as they all were. But who had done it better in every way not only for himself but for them than their good old friend Arshak Sarkies? What would Penang do without him? And that night the crown had been put upon his work in perhaps the finest hotel in the East (Applause). Not only had he done good work in public, but in private his left hand had done many a good deed of which his right knew nothing. For his actions both public and private he was a man of whom Penang and the Straits and the whole of Malaya should be proud. If

Advertisement from the *Official Guide for Shippers and Travellers to the Principal Ports of the World*, produced by Osaka Shosen Kaisha, edited by M. Franklin Kline 1927–8.
By courtesy of the Penang State Library

Extract from *The Penang Gazette*, Weekly Mail Edition, Wednesday 3rd January, 1923.
This is the speech given by Arshak Sarkies on the occasion of the January 1st opening of the E and O ballroom.
By courtesy of the Penang State Library

determinations of *de rigueur* dress, so that the popularity of dancing remained undiminished even after the guns were thundering in the west.

Police regulations requiring that balls end at midnight must have been a bit of a dampener, but apparently on special occasions such as New Year's Eve extensions to 2.00 am were granted.

Mrs Dorothy Downe, a missionary's daughter, recalling at the age of 84 her attendance at the Raffles dances when she was in her twenties, said it was hard nowadays to imagine the strictness of life. The waltz and the valita were still in vogue; the one-step and two-step were new. The Charleston did not hit Singapore until the late 1920s.

"It was very formal—we had to check off our dance engagements on little programmes. We had good bands brought out from Britain. The dancing was mainly in the dining room at first, since the present dance floor was then just an open verandah," she added.

The new ballroom, often referred to as "the coolest ballroom in the East", was in fact opened on the verandah fronting Beach Road in the mid-1920s, with the Long Bar, snake-shape, intertwining the columns of the lobby. According to one habitué, Brian "Buck" Buckeridge, a former fire service chief, a dancer could sit on the ballroom floor with his hand on the garden fence.

Another old-timer, James Gagan, who arrived in Singapore in 1922, said that girls were still in short supply—"You would merely *hope* to dance"—and that Cad's Alley, the passageway still flanking the ballroom and present Long Bar area, got its name because "You sat there at the bar, waiting, and if your friend had a girl-friend on the dance floor, he couldn't leave the table, or he would lose her!"

It was out of the question for a European to attempt to take a local "native" girl into the hotel, let alone on the dance floor. Not only would it be cause for scandalised gossip and social ostracism, besides a reprimand from his boss at the office, but in most cases, the "culprit" would be sent straight home on the boat to England in disgrace.

Even the Eurasian was barred from most clubs and hotels of that time. One Eurasian says he feels uncomfortable to this day when entering former European strongholds such as the Tanglin Club or the Raffles Hotel. This was why the Eurasians had their own club, the Singapore Recreation Club, facing the Singapore Cricket Club at the other end of the Padang cricket pitch; even to this day the membership of this club is predominantly Eurasian.

That the hotel was a social centre as much, if not more, for Singapore residents as for hotel guests, can be gauged from the fact that most of the diners and dancers were apparently regulars. "You didn't even have to book a table," says one who was among them in those days. "Everyone knew their places already. They were regular, came every week."

With the verandah ballroom exposed to public view on the Beach Road side, the spectacle of the Europeans enjoying themselves in this eccentric and morally outrageous manner (men holding women in their arms for the waltz and so on) became one of the cheapest shows in town for the locals.

The reaction of the spectators is enlightening. Mr Ong Chin Hai, a shopkeeper who used to supply the hotel with rubber matting and similar furnishing, is typical. He had just come of age in 1922, newly arrived and still a country greenhorn from China's southern Fukien province.

"We would all squat on the opposite side, on the football pitches in Beach Road, and stare all night into the ballroom, where the Europeans were dancing. I had never seen anything like it, and they were wearing tails. And every Saturday night, there was free cinema in the ballroom too," he said, his arm imitating the winding gesture of the old cinematographic operators.

Another custom which amazed locals was the "chit" system of getting drinks on credit, in heavy use by most Europeans. An Asian newspaper editor showed how it was viewed. Surveying the hotel scene he said that of the 500 to 600 guests, probably not five possessed more than a single dollar note in their pockets. None would pass money. After three to six months, all the chits collected at the hotel would be sent on.

Some people did not pay for a long time and some did not pay at all. There was, he asserted, one man who owed the hotel between eight and nine thousand dollars who was still signing chits.

This was a far cry from 1899, when the *Straits Times* denounced a new-fangled system, permitting guests to lay out a deposit and get drinks for chits issued against it, as a "cumbersome and unhappy way of getting a drink", and expressed the hope that people would be able to carry about with them as much money as would serve to quench their thirst.

It seems that far too many husbands were busy with work upcountry ("outstation" as it is still called today in Singapore), or perhaps playing sports, always to escort their wives and daughters to the dances, particularly the early evening tea dances between 6-00 pm and 6.30 pm which became popular in the later 1920s and 1930s. This was a boon to the many footloose bachelors in search of dancing partners and no doubt the start of many an extramarital flirtation.

But rarely more than a flirtation, according to Malayan civil servant Victor Purcell in his memoirs, *pace* novelist Somerset Maugham's tales of torrid intrigue.

He thought that cheek-to-cheek encounters on the darkened dance-floor and "that symbolic parlour game known to its votaries as footy-footy, were more common than actual adultery". Other observers thought that the social *mores* were causing nervous disorders, or at the very least, prurient, repressed sexuality. But gossipy Singapore found no difficulty in magnifying the slightest flirtation and this was all grist to the mill for the inquisitive Somerset Maugham, a Raffles "regular" in the 1920s and 1930s, who was despised by his victims as an ingrate snooper of the worst order.

The Johor Causeway linking Singapore with mainland Malaya opened in 1923, and, with the 1920–23 rubber slump behind and tin prices soaring, the upcountry planters, estate managers and tin mine-owners were becoming an important source of custom to the Raffles, motoring long distances from the hinterland to enjoy the comforts of urban life. Invariably one of their objects was to find a dance floor partner, who often, in Lockhart's words, would be "the wife of some official or businessman who prefers his bridge and his 'stengah' to the gyrations of a one-step".

Like the oilmen of the 1960s and 1970s, the planters of the 1920s and 1930s were out for a good time after the privations of remote jungle plantations where, as Doris Geddes of the boutique in Raffles Hotel said, "They slept on nothing but bare boards, after which anything was heaven".

Although Purcell, who seems to have disagreed on most things with Somerset Maugham, said that the whisky-swilling planters were a figment of the journalist's imagination, it seems likely they were heavy-drinking men and generally self-indulgent to a point which must have drawn many a disapproving look from the memsahibs. After all, a *whisky ayer* (whisky water) was only about 25 cents at the Raffles then (which was slightly more expensive than the usual 20 cents elsewhere). And Lockhart caustically condemned the expatriate's propensity for alcohol as being "mainly responsible for that absence of intellectual interests which is a defective feature of British colonial life in tropical countries".

But the Sarkies knew which side their business bread was buttered on, for the planters and their like were big spenders—a month in the hotel worked out at about $180 all in then, when $1 was equivalent to about the old half-crown—even if the management did have to give them extended credit during slumps.

"There's just one rule here," the tolerant Arshak Sarkies told a guest at the time. "We ring the bell at six o'clock in the morning and you all go back to your own rooms."

Somerset Maugham painted a depressing picture of the typical planter in *A Writer's Notebook* under the entries for 1922 and 1929:

> "He has been out for 10 years. He is a bachelor. . . . There is something pathetic about him. He lives alone in a very untidy bungalow. On the walls are innumerable pictures of women in all states of undress," and "The greater number of them are rough and common men of something below the middle class and they speak English with a vile accent or broad Scotch. They have vulgar minds, occupied only with rubber and its price and the sports of their club . . . You would have to go far to find among the planters a man of culture, reading or distinction."

This may have been true, for Bilainikin noted in 1932 that there were over 1,000 illiterate Europeans in the Straits Settlements, with one illiterate in seven Europeans in Johor, the Malayan state closest to Singapore.

Rowdyism almost invariably occurred after a sports match against a visiting team, a typical example of boisterous behaviour occurring in 1926 when both teams, having dined well at the Cricket Club, invaded Raffles at a late hour and a few bright spirits finally took over the band. The resident drummer, monocled

Vaughan Jones, a local celebrity known to his large circle of admirers simply by his initials, V. J., was unceremoniously pushed on one side and listened in amused astonishment to his instruments being forced to produce a volume of discordant sound that woke guests in their beds and must have made some of them wonder whether an artillery barrage was taking place.

The closure of the Hotel de l'Europe in the mid-1930s finally assured the Raffles's position as the colony's social centre, for tourists and for planters down from the Federated Malay States for relaxation and jollification.

The hotel was fortunate in being able to obtain occasional extension by a couple of hours of the closing time ordained as a result of what one critic called "a Victorian conception of when its inhabitants should be in bed". Thus dancing and drinking were allowed to take place beyond the puritanical hour of midnight. Paradoxically it was on Saturdays that this bacchanalian revelry was permitted, the authorities perhaps overlooking the fact that it resulted in the Sabbath being invaded and curtailed. Apart from Raffles, Singapore was as dead at midnight on all seven days of the week as a village in pietistic Scotland or Wales on the day devoted to rest and religious observance.

By this time, of course, the Raffles had passed from the Sarkies family's hands with the demise of the last of the brothers, Arshak, and the subsequent bankruptcy case in 1931. But the family continued to have a stake in the business, as did the Armenian manager, Martyrose Sarkies Arathoon, until the Second World War.

The depression of the early 1930s hit the hotel hard, but it never closed, as many other hotels did. Times were also changing, with nationalist and revolutionary activity in China spilling over into Singapore. Singapore recovered economically however, and on the surface at least, life continued very much as usual.

The hotel apparently had 120 rooms in 1934 and underwent some renovation at about that time. Electrically powered refrigeration rooms were installed for storage of food, which had until then been cooled by blocks of ice. The management was particularly proud of its newly modernised bathrooms, with red and white towels, long baths, blue shower rooms and running hot and cold water.

Like all innovations that replace quaint local customs, these de luxe facilities were not received without nostalgic sighs from guests who had known the hotel since the turn of the century for the old three-foot tall "Shanghai jar"—also known as the "Siamese" or "Java" jar—from which a person performed his ablutions by panning water in a scoop to sluice himself down, Malay-style. Many had been the jokes about new arrivals, greenhorns or old ladies, who, confronted with this alien "bath", had bravely attempted to climb into the jar and promptly got stuck.

There were also some electrical improvements—cube lighting in the dining room, illuminated pylons in the Palm Court and colour flooding for the ballroom.

THE DANCING YEARS

It was in the 1930s that the fabled snobbery and racism of the British Empire really took root, only a symptom of the inner rot and decline that was to lead to its diminution, if not total disappearance, after the Second World War.

The role of white women in the now highly stratified society of Singapore has already been noted. So has the influence of revolutionary and anti-foreign unrest in China. Across the road from the hotel, the locals still stared in at the Europeans, perhaps with less curiosity and wonderment than in the 1920s, but with more anger and resentment.

The Sarkies had run their hotel in the grand style typical of their era; but forces beyond their control—and beyond the shores of Singapore—were gathering, forces which would put an end to their lavish, almost foolishly generous, style of hospitality. The colony's way of life never fully recovered, despite a false remission in the mid-1930s, and the dark clouds of war closed in on it.

So divorced from reality, so aging and eccentric, had Arshak, the last Sarkies, become, holed up hermit-like at the E and O hotel in Penang, that as the 1930s drew nigh and he himself entered his sixties he chose to embark on an opulent reconstruction of both E and O and the Sea View in Singapore at the precise moment when Singapore began to enter an economic slump. He committed himself to this folly when tin prices were soaring and there was over-production of rubber—a situation which bred false confidence.

The Sarkies hotels' reliance on the planter and miner clientele has been mentioned. So have Arshak's zany streak of generosity, his penchant for horse racing and the prevalence of the "pay later" hotel chit system among European patrons. There was but one ingredient lacking to complete this recipe for ruin, and that was duly supplied in the shape of the world depression of the early 1930s. Between 1929 and 1932, rubber prices slid from an average of 34 cents a pound to a mere 4.95 cents.

Suddenly Arshak's hotels were flooded with planters from up country looking for jobs and hoping to sponge on him until there was a turn for the better. But Arshak was already up to his neck in loans. The bank began to smell a rat and insultingly insisted that he appoint a European accountant at the E and O. In desperation he turned to that ancient last resort, the money-lender.

He was charged ludicrously high interest rates but the loans were conveniently unsecured by any collateral. And Arshak was not pulling in his belt to help ward off disaster. His entertainment account was now about $14,000 a year, which even his partner Arathoon later agreed was "excessive". Friends, bandsmen and other peripheral employees of the company were all staying free at his hotels. He had even advanced personal loans to racehorse trainers.

Arathoon for his part had apparently failed to control the almost feudal distribution of favour and graft among the Raffles staff, especially among the Hainanese Chinese "Mafia" that dominated it; there was a rumour that the "boy" in charge of the bar was paying $1,000 a month for the privilege of working there, so attractive was his rake-off from the takings which rightfully should have gone into the hotel kitty.

Mr Arshak Sarkies. *Straits Produce*, 1 July 1929. By courtesy of the Library of the Royal Commonwealth Society

Meanwhile, Arshak was quarrelling incessantly with Arathoon, who was highly critical of his management of the books (professional outsiders were later to vindicate his opinion), and the pair of them were concurrently engaged in bitter running fights with the widows and families of Arshak's brothers.

Arathoon felt, perhaps understandably, that the Raffles's fixed and unrealised assets, combined with its undoubted earning potential, far outweighed its liabilities. But while he stoutly maintained that cash, not a shortage of assets, was the main problem, auditors pointed out that the black, in fact, fell short of the red by at least $2.5 million.

Indeed the hotel business generally, once so extravagantly flourishing, had fallen on evil days. Arathoon had been declared bankrupt, the hotel company's true plight having been exposed for all to see during almost two weeks' court proceedings, although the creditors at first did their utmost to exclude the press from their own meetings.

Throughout the court proceedings in 1931 Arathoon had continued as the manager of the Raffles, with an allowance and board and lodging for himself, his wife, two daughters and a son. Although he was now given notice, it proved

Mr M. S. Arathoon.
By courtesy of the Library
of the Royal Commonwealth Society

impossible to get rid of him, so thoroughly did he understand the hotel's labyrinthine affairs. He and his son stayed on as book-keepers, even as assistant managers, during the Japanese occupation of 1942–1945.

A new company, Raffles Hotel Ltd, was incorporated in February 1933. Naturally, it was considered necessary to create as "bullish" an atmosphere as possible if it was to prosper and the board was greatly assisted in this by the revival of world economic confidence and Singapore's own recovery from the slump. The first chairman, Evan Nuttall Taylor, had no compunction at all in equating any lack of confidence in the Raffles with virtual treason against Singapore itself. "The measure of your faith in the shares which you hold in Raffles must be the measure of your faith in the colony," he declared.

The British were soon hastily setting up their naval base and fortifications in Singapore, the Japanese having occupied Manchuria in 1931 and then proceeding over the course of the next few years to withdraw from several international conventions. The price of land was soaring and the Raffles board was cock-a-hoop at the news that the Government had acquired the site of the Europe Hotel, setting the seal on the demise of an old rival. The Supreme Court and City Hall now stand on that site, fronting the Padang cricket ground.

4 SAMURAI IN THE PALM COURT

By 1940 the Raffles Hotel board was urging the Government to publicise the tourist attractions of Malaya more vigorously, because the outbreak of the Second World War had already stunted the tourist trade.

Although the Raffles management said it had prepared an air-raid shelter (alleged by some to be a "pathetic tin-roofed hut" near the storeroom, incapable of withstanding the shock of more than a small anti-aircraft splinter), extra water tanks should the municipal supply be shut off, and fire-fighting equipment, it obviously did not see the war as a long-term threat, least of all as relevant to the future of the hotel.

The board chairman, James Clarke, told the annual general meeting in June 1941, less than eight months before the Japanese took Singapore: "I fully realise this is certainly not the time to talk of inviting tourists to Malaya, but I trust that when peace has been restored to the world, Malaya's claims as a place of interest will not be overlooked, and that Government when that time comes will take the necessary practical steps to encourage tourist traffic here . . ."

Yet the signs were unmistakeable: the British were busily making of Singapore what they fondly imagined was an impregnable fortress. Singapore was thronged with military and there were more uniforms than evening dress at the Raffles's dances which went on till midnight.

Like the inhabitants of many other colonial outposts, however, white Singaporeans gave what at best was but a lukewarm welcome to the overseas servicemen who disembarked on their soil in the early days of the war. The innate snobbery that characterised the "white settler" mentality extended beyond racial discrimination and erected class barriers against even European "other ranks". Even though these gallant but, some said, green young men had been posted to defend one of the bastions of the British Empire, the Raffles and Singapore maintained a snooty distance from them. The Raffles posted military police outside its doors to keep the non-officers out.

Particularly resentful of this insensitivity were the Australians. One of them was Russell Braddon, then a humble gunner but later to become a celebrated author, and he has recounted in his book *The Naked Island* how he ignored the "out of bounds" sign at the Raffles to carry a letter of introduction from his grandmother to a woman guest who, not immediately realising his identity, asked a drinks waiter to tell "that soldier" to leave. When he relayed his message requesting her to "go to hell" she told the waiter to send for the "Red Caps" and to bring Mr Braddon to have a drink with her. He walked over, told her who he was and said: "I wouldn't drink here or anywhere else with you. And when this war with Japan starts and you go screeching off on the first evacuation ship to Australia, I sincerely hope that none of my family will either."

Contrite, she attempted to apologise and asked where he was going. He told her: "To Lavender Street (the brothel quarter)—the Green Cat. Down there the women are bitches and they know it. I think I prefer it that way."

Later Braddon heard that the woman was drowned when one of the last evacuee ships left Singapore harbour. "Apparently she had been very brave. During most of that four years, of course, Raffles was a Japanese brothel," he observed sardonically. Braddon was repeating what was apparently an untrue rumour; there is ample evidence that the Raffles was never used by the Japanese army for what was known by the military as a "comfort station" for the troops. Mamoru Shinokazi, the administrator in charge of Singapore during the occupation, said it was strictly forbidden to take any girl into the hotel at that time. Mr Swee and other hotel workers stoutly maintained that the Japanese Officers were upright men—strict disciplinarians, but, provided they were not provoked, fair in their dealings with the staff.

Even junior-ranking young British civil servants could hardly afford to frequent the Raffles in those days and the Asians, naturally, did not get any better deal.

Leo Jenkins, a Malayan planter, signed up in the army but found that he and his friends, all raw cadets-in-training, were not exactly welcomed by the cliquish regulars. "Why should we equip them?" shouted the Colonel to the adjutant, "We haven't got enough for our own men." When they went to the adjutant after receiving their uniforms and kit and asked when he wanted to see them again, he said, "I don't want to see you again", and added with a slight smile, "ever".

"So we, all fully equipped and dressed as privates, went and spent our period of service in our old haunt, the Raffles Hotel!" said Perky.

Characters such as Leo and his mates, as well as the swelling tide of refugees from up-country Malaya, served only to overcrowd the Raffles. Still, as a former member of that respected breed, the Malayan planters, Perky got VIP treatment despite his low starting rank of private. On one occasion he cashed a cheque at the desk and an officer next to him was to his chagrin and indignation refused a similar request. The officer exclaimed: "But you have just cashed one for that private!" and Perky walked quickly away before any explanation could be offered.

The complacency of the colony's defenders matched the snobbery of its civilian population—and retribution waited in the wings. Unremarked by most Singapore residents, the civilian Japanese population of Malaya had by 1940 reached about 8,000, with almost half resident in Singapore. A large number of them clustered around the Raffles itself, running textile shops in Middle Road, Hylam Street and Malay Street. There was a Japanese fishermen's *kampong* or village at Bedok, a seaside suburb, where Marine Parade is today. Decorative paper fish could be seen fluttering in the breeze whenever a new baby was born in the new settlement. At Katong suburb, there was a Japanese seaside clubhouse complete with geisha girls. And along the coast was dotted a string of small Japanese-run hotels.

The commercial activities of the Japanese, whose goods filled the Chinese shops as well as their own, was a focus for resentment among the competitive local Chinese, especially after the Japanese had attacked China in 1937.

Not all the Japanese were engaged on innocent business, despite their "cover" stories. They were mainly to be found running iron mines in Malaya (useful for strategic materials, some remarked), as well as a few rubber estates, and a mass of shops, street stalls, massage parlours and dental clinics in Singapore. Very many were photographers; in fact, it was almost impossible to get a passport photograph taken after their internment as enemy nationals at the end of 1941, so thorough was their monopoly of this business.

Many of the Japanese traders and fishermen who left before the war started came back as army officers with specific information on the entire population of the island. Certain of the photographers were undoubtedly agents who had been planted by Tokyo.

One photographer who was in an ideal position to obtain valuable information, Shigesaburo Nakajima, actually ran the studio in Raffles Shopping Arcade. He had been busy before the war taking pictures at all the military balls at the hotel and therefore was in an ideal position to build up a huge dossier on senior Allied army officers. Whether he actually did so will never be known for

Japan Club Sports Day 1930.
In front of the Raffles, as seen from the beach by photographer Toyosaburo Ishizu, nephew of Nakajima whose studios were in the hotel shopping arcade—one of the many signs of a growing Japanese pre-war presence in Malaya.
By courtesy of Toyosaburo Ishizu

The photo studio, once run by Nakajima and his nephews in the 1930s, is still there, to the back of the hotel, off Bras Basah Road.
From the author's collection.

certain. He was in his late fifties at the time, and left his nephews Noboru Nakajima and Toyosaburo Ishizu to manage the business when he quit the island before the Japanese occupation and went to Shanghai. Toyosaburo, the last of the family to leave, was caught and interned in India.

Shinozaki, who much endeared himself to his Singaporean charges, described tales of Nakajima and his like being spies as "nonsense", but most detached observers are convinced that there was in fact a carefully established espionage network in existence of which Shinozaki was not necessarily aware.

Tan Geok Swee, who retired in 1980 as chief cashier at the Raffles, where he had worked since 1936, said in an interview not long after leaving the hotel that he was certain of this.

"I found the transformation of people who had seemed to be humble street traders into swaggering army officers quite incredible", he said.

The presence of Allied troops, the anti-aircraft gun stationed outside the Raffles—which attracted much attention from Japanese news reporters—, the siren tests every Saturday morning, regular drill at their headquarters opposite the hotel by the Straits Settlements Volunteers (the first half-hearted attempt to recruit Asians to the colony's defence, since their capacity for battle was doubted by the whites), frequent fire practices and the huge and protective presence of the mighty naval base, all helped to create a false sense of security in the minds of Singapore's Europeans.

Europeans at the Raffles' one-time sister hotel, the Sea View—where everyone who was anyone spent their Sunday mornings in those days—, and no doubt in the Raffles itself, were cheerfully singing "There'll always be an England", to wind up their tiffin or sundowner drinks. Business was as usual.

Particularly when it came to dancing. As late as Christmas 1941, when the Japanese had already started bombing Singapore from their by now well entrenched bases in Malaya, and the Raffles management had been obliged to set up a blackout around the huge ballroom, couples danced in evening dress between the raids. Often the would-be revellers had literally to fumble their way across the dance floor, bumping into each other and stepping on one another's toes. But the show went doggedly on till midnight. Amazingly, right into January 1942 you still had to book a table.

Up on the roof sat the hotel engineer, on watch. Four whistles from him was the danger signal, usually meaning that the droning enemy planes were already directly overhead and readying to drop their bombs.

Fortunately the hotel was not painted pure white then, as it is now; it was dark green and white, with gaily striped window awnings to match—this broken colour scheme may have acted as camouflage to make it a less obvious target from the air. Or it may be, as some have said, that the Japanese wanted to keep the Raffles for themselves right from the start.

To many of the guests, however, the air-raids amounted to little more than an infernal nuisance, an unwelcome interruption to their dinner. As the local staff, often led by the more craven Europeans, usually scattered in all directions and abandoned the scene at the first hoot of the sirens, those intrepid few who remained were often forced to plunder the kitchens for themselves, by the light of a torch. Not everyone paid his bill on such occasions. At the Sea View guests were offering the American pilots billeted there a bottle of champagne for every Japanese plane shot down.

Two dances in particular stood out during these grey days. The first was on 10 December 1941, when the news came that the Japanese had sunk off Malaya the great British battleships the *Prince of Wales* and the *Repulse*, and with them all hope for Singapore. The hotel's ballroom verandah cleared immediately as though, in the words of journalist Noel Barber, "the last waltz had just been played". This was the beginning of the end.

The second was the last dance before the British surrender to the Japanese on 15 February 1942. The Raffles did not really keep on dancing right up to that date—there probably was a 9.00 pm curfew for at least 10 days before—but certainly the last dance was an occasion enshrined in memory as a fine example of the British "stiff upper lip".

In fire service chief "Buck" Buckeridge's words, it was "like a football match, everyone jampacked on the ballroom floor, with nowhere else to go, all the Singapore volunteers disbanded and advised to get out of civvies and so on. It was highly jovial. There was no idea of a fall—the idea was not prevalent, anyway. I myself did not believe it until I put my wife on a ship out, on February 9."

And Leo Jenkins says, "I remember watching a great dance, the last that was held in the hotel before the fall of Singapore. How gay the ladies, the smiles and laughter, how beautiful the dresses and smart the white mess kits of the officers! I remember remarking to one of my companions. 'This must be just like the Duchess of Richmond's ball before the battle of Waterloo!'"

It was a long way from the Raffles ballroom to the Japanese "Death Railway" in Thailand, where Leo soon found himself working under barbaric conditions for four years. Yet he testified for the defence of Colonel Yanagida, officer in charge of Camp Number Two, where he had been consigned, at a war crimes trial after the 1945 liberation. As a result, the colonel's death sentence was commuted to 14 years' imprisonment, and finally cut short at only three years. For years afterwards, Perky kept up a friendly correspondence with the grateful Yanagida family.

The end of the chit system in January 1942 had already confirmed Singapore residents' worst fears; but they really knew it was curtains when the Governor ordered them to pour one of their most precious possessions straight down the drain: a total ban on liquor was announced on February 13, in an effort to avoid the drunken pillage and rape in which the Japanese had indulged when taking Hongkong. Needless to say, most people kept back a bottle or two "just in case", and buried or hid them somewhere. At the Raffles, the Armenian (unofficial) manager, Arathoon, was extremely reluctant to obey the order. He finally steeled himself to pour some of the drink away; the hotel stank of expensive brandies and liqueurs for weeks afterwards. The British, incidentally, paid compensation after the war for this loss.

Lovingly, the staff carefully buried the magnificent silver roast beef trolley in the Palm Court, denying "the Nips" this pride and joy of the typical British colonial table. As the end drew near and the Japanese advanced, now actually on Singapore soil, Europeans gathered at the Raffles almost as a reflex action, huddling in the rundown corridors of their one-time playground. Their washing lines were strung untidily across the ballroom.

Dorothy Downe, then 48, recalled a scene of nightmare neglect and devastation: "I spent my last night of freedom at the hotel. If chaos can be empty, then that would describe the hotel at that time. Not a soul there actually belonged to the hotel. All the rooms were in turmoil, the cupboards open, clothes flung around."

Dorothy had been working at the General Hospital as an emergency nurse until it was decided she was too old to go on, and should go to the Raffles, as the Japanese had instructed, on pain of being shot. "Two of us tumbled into a room on the Bras Basah side. Taps turned off, no food. Next day, we started walking to

The famous silver roast beef trolley.
By courtesy of the Raffles Hotel; photograph taken by the Raffles Photographers, for the manager

Katong (a good hour's walk). Some British officers stopped in a car and gave us a lift. I gave one of them a jade ring for his girl, but I never saw him again and don't know his name."

Lucia Bach, another Briton, then 45, headed for the Raffles kitchen when she got to the hotel. As the daughter of a long-term expatriate engineer and mosquito-control officer (whom the Japanese later executed), she had been surrounded from childhood by Asian servants, so "I had never cooked. I hadn't the faintest idea what to do. I just inspected it for cleanliness, and found it crawling with cockroaches."

Most Europeans behaved well, but among some of them the usual codes of polite behaviour, formerly so strictly enforced in stuffy colonial Singapore, broke down under the stress. Lucia clearly remembers one guest, a middle-aged widow, generously inviting others to share her room at the Raffles. These others, however, were invariably young bachelors. "Sometimes, she would make love with her lover right in front of them all, while they slept on her floor", Lucia asserted.

According to Lucia too, the Governor, Sir Shenton Thomas, assumed charge while among the trembling band of Europeans in the hotel. When the Japanese arrived at the hotel, his face was slapped in front of all the others and he was asked: "Who are you to give orders? You're not the Governor any more."

"We were all very cowed by that", says Lucia.

And so they set off to their internment at Changi Prison, or to Thailand—and, for many, to their death.

Former assistant manager Ernest Smith was taken prisoner at the Volunteers' headquarters opposite the hotel. The Italian manager, Guido Cevenini, had already left Singapore and been interned as an enemy national in Australia, but had handed over to Ernest his family heirlooms—priceless earrings, brooches and rings, set with emeralds and diamonds. Ernest took them out of the hotel safe and marched to Changi with them.

"At Changi, we were told to hand over any valuables in our possession, to give to the Japanese, for safe-keeping. I had Guido's Leica camera with me too. That same night, I found three tins at the engineering sheds, RAF Changi, and so I put the camera in one of them, taped the lid on, and put it inside the two other tins, wrapped in a rubber groundsheet. In the dead of night, I buried it on a hillside by the barracks at the risk of the guard seeing me, or being shot. I buried it three feet down.

"But the jewellery I kept on me. We were told if we were caught doing this, we would be shot. I suppose this didn't register with me at the time. I got the jewellery to Thailand, to the railway. We were issued with wooden clogs . . . and my friend, a carpenter, hollowed out the clog soles and fitted plugs, smoothing them over to make a tight fit. I got another pair made to wear, but the jewellery I put in this pair. I put some more of it in a powdered milk tin with a false bottom made by the same man. I kept water in the tin all the time, as though it was a drinking receptacle, to explain the extra weight. The guards did pick up the clogs once—the agony I went through!

"Finally, I got them back to Guido, after the War. A fortnight after we got back, we went to that Changi hillside with our *changkols* (a kind of local pickaxe) and at the first point we dug, we found the tin! The camera had deteriorated so that only the lens was worth anything. But Guido danced around like a lunatic and shouted, 'It's not possible! Not possible!' He had the lens put into another camera. He could hardly believe the jewellery was still safe either, and offered me part of it. I had the jewellery valued in the UK, at £55,000!"

After the British prisoners had vacated the hotel, and dispersed to their various fates in February 1942, German and Italian civilians were brought in from Outram Prison where they had been interned by the British.

Finally, the Japanese demonstrated that they knew a good thing when they saw one: the Raffles was promptly commandeered by Imperial Army Headquarters (Transport and Supplies Section) for the use of high ranking Japanese officers only—still too high-class a venue for "other ranks". Most of the new "guests" were on short-term transit. They stayed free of charge, except for drinks, for which they had to pay. The hotel was rarely fully booked those days.

The new "management", led by an army paymaster, set about rounding up the old Singapore staff, who had fled, and cleaning up the building. The hotel's immediate occupation by the Japanese military police had however saved it from any really serious looting.

The next person after the Governor to feel the sting of a Japanese slap was Arathoon, who at first foolishly and stubbornly refused to hand over the key to the storeroom where the confectionery, flour, sugar and no doubt the balance of the hotel's cellar was stacked. But he was kept on, together with the Eurasian maitre d'hotel, G. Attias, who had enough Italian blood in him to satisfy the Japanese, but was still expected to wear the red arm-band which marked out all the hotel staff as enemy personnel.

There was a running tussle throughout the occupation between the staff and certain Japanese who had been pre-war visitors to the hotel, and who remembered all too well that, somewhere, there should be a silver roast-beef trolley . . .

Japanese reaction to "provocation" however could be brutal: when the cook stole eggs for himself, he was tied to a tree-trunk in the Palm Court and beaten black and blue by the Japanese as they passed by, almost in sport. Some unfortunates, like the Eurasian storekeeper, William James Collick, were blamed for thefts, when certain of the Japanese themselves had in fact removed stocks to sell on the lucrative Singapore black market, where a bottle of whisky was going for $12,000, a tin of butter for $950.

More seriously, one Chinese roomboy who offended them, a 50-year-old opium addict, underwent the "Japanese water torture" in a backroom off the

Elizabethan Grill. "His face was like a pumpkin afterwards", Tan Geok Swee recalled. The Japanese interrogators filled his stomach with water, then jumped on it.

Tan also remembers that there were two officers from the dreaded Kempeitai secret police stationed at the Raffles, who kept a close watch on the staff.

There was a minor crisis soon after the Japanese arrived: most of the officers fell sick with food poisoning severe enough to cause ugly skin rashes. Tan Geok Swee said it was caused by fish which had been polluted by the dead bodies floating in the harbour, victims of the Japanese massacres of the Chinese.

This incident caused some suffering for the hotel staff, since the Japanese were already so suspicious that they would hardly drink a cup of coffee without asking the waiter to taste it first, for fear it might be poisoned.

For the most part, however, the staff quickly adjusted to what amounted to little more than serving a new master, with only a few variations on the preoccupation theme, some of which they even found quite interesting. The hotel was now renamed Syonan Ryokan (Hotel Syonan, after Singapore, now also called Syonan, meaning "Light of the South" in Japanese). And the Elizabethan Grill became simply the Japanese Inn.

Another physical change, was the moving of the entrance from the natural "front" of the hotel, off the ballroom verandah, at the western corner of Beach Road-Bras Basah Road, to the Beach Road side where it is now.

Possibly, the Japanese decided to block off the old entrance because they found it, and the open verandah, insecure—too open to the potentially hostile, and certainly nosy, Singapore public.

Bemused roomboys, more used to the decorously over-dressed British, had now to accustom themselves to the spectacle of half-naked Japanese samurai lounging in their loincloths, or less, and whirling huge broad-bladed swords around their heads while drilling in the Palm Court.

"They used to squat on the chairs—they had no European manners", remarked Tan Geok Swee, with obvious distaste. He and his colleagues learned to bow to the Japanese and to their flag, to assemble early in the morning at the ballroom for physical jerks and the Japanese national anthem while bowing to the east, to set the clocks on Tokyo time, to speak, cook and eat Japanese, and, more than ever before, to do as they were told.

From Tokyo, Japanese managers, cooks and young girl housekeepers, all army personnel, were flown out to supplement the local hotel staff.

Japanese cooks provided simple Japanese dishes, such as *miso* soup and rice for breakfast. The officers drank *sake* and Kirin beer, but few Singaporeans got anything better than rice beer or Nanboku "whisky", made from fermented pineapples. There were no menus and no room service.

Mr Applebaum and his Hungarian orchestra, from the Adelphi Hotel, provided the "cabaret", playing Japanese songs such as "*Aikoku Koshinkyoku*" —"Behold the dawn in the east over the sea; the morning sun shines high in the sky, fresh spirits above and below on earth; there leaps the hope of Great Japan"—and Western classical music.

While the Japanese were thus distracted, the staff would cluster round Swiss maitre d'hotel Henry Wallter Gachnang, to hear the latest war news from the world outside. As a citizen of neutral Switzerland. Gachnang could come and go as he pleased and listen outside—at the Red Cross, for instance—to the radio broadcasts which the Japanese had forbidden to ordinary folk, on pain of instant decapitation.

There was still the occasional function at the Raffles—one big and very hush-hush party was held for the crew of a top-secret German submarine which came into port, but who did not stay at the hotel itself. Another was hosted in May 1944 by Colonel Iwakuro, Japanese intelligence chief for the region, to entertain representatives of the Indian Independence League and Indian National Army officers, Indian nationalists who had thrown in their lot with the Japanese.

Among other known guests during this period were Mr N. Toshima, the Japanese in charge of the Chinese in Java, and General Tojo himself, the Premier of Japan. The Japanese seemed to have little difficulty mustering a good spread for such occasions, though perhaps not quite as sumptuous as in the good old days. Some of it may have come from the nearby Raffles Institution's schoolfields, which the Japanese had ploughed up to plant tapioca and vegetables. Staff say the Japanese would also slaughter pigs in the hotel.

The staff began to gather from their clandestine radio-listening that things were not going all the Japanese way. Certainly this was clear by 1945, when disorder was visible in Singapore, with food shortages fuelling an uncontrollable black market. Many hotel staff had been press-ganged into hard labour to build air-raid shelters—the Palm Court itself was pockmarked with trenches and shelter holes. By July that year, Allied planes were to be seen over Singapore, and the hotel shook to the vibrations of bombing at the old Kallang Airport nearby.

Hearing the news of Japan's defeat in Rangoon, in May 1945, at least one Japanese officer staying at the Raffles committed *hara-kiri*—ritual suicide by disembowelment—in one of the rooms on the Bras Basah Road side, which were reserved mainly for airforce officers. True to the Samurai concept of honour, he left a note explaining that he had taken his own life and that the Chinese should not be blamed for it.

Abruptly, the Japanese vacated the hotel on September 4. Arathoon and his son, despite their ill health, at once assembled the staff and proudly opened the hotel to the public on the following day. The first arrivals found the pages of the hotel register which would have shown the names of the Japanese "guests", neatly torn out.

Soon afterwards, the former hotel engineer, Mr James, made his way from internment in Changi to report for duty. He was later publicly commended by the board chairman for this devotion to his job, with "a word for the Asiatic staff" too.

Before long, the hotel had became a transit point for Allied army personnel returning to their posts, and for a skeletal, tattered army of refugees—shaking

SAMURAI IN THE PALM COURT

and covered in sores—emerging from internment camps with tales of horror and deprivation. Many of them burst into tears when they saw the familiar façade of the Raffles once more. There was a rush for the bathrooms, for what was, for most of them, the first bath in many years.

Gone was the hotel's former gracious style, maintained to some extent even during the Japanese occupation: now guests had to share their rooms with from three to six others. The food was condemned even by ex-internees as "bloody awful", and it was tinned, and expensive to boot. People slept on the floors, six and more to a room, and ate tinned carrots for breakfast. Others had to try to obtain a night's rest on the billiards tables. The ballroom was out of commission for at least six months and there was precious little to drink at the bar.

The 1946 annual general meeting, which phlegmatically reported on the events of 1942 as though there had been only some minor interruption, assessed trading profits for March 1941 to August 1946 at $457,953. The report tut-tutted about the ravages of the occupation, recording "loss and deterioration of our kitchen equipment and failure of our hot water system due to the carelessness of the enemy occupants".

That old habits die hard was proved in September 1945. Although the hotel had every reason to be grateful to all Allied uniformed personnel, officers or not, Charles Taylor, then serving in HMS *Providence*, a British minesweeper, once again came smack up against the "class bar".

Although "immaculate in our tropical white uniforms", and eager to sample the fabled luxuries of the famous hotel, Taylor and his shipmates—after waiting 20 minutes for a waiter to appear—were quizzed by him as to their exact rank when they tried to order a legendary gin sling and the only item then on the menu, sausages and mash.

"Are the gentlemen of the rank of lieutenant-colonel or its equivalent?" asked the waiter.

"No", they said, "but please convey our compliments to the manager and inform him that we are devotees of Somerset Maugham and rejoice in the tradition of Raffles." The waiter retired, only to return with the reply that since they were not of the required rank, he could not serve them, and they must leave at once.

As they trooped disconsolately out, Taylor exclaimed more in amusement than irritation, "My God!—peace has broken out!"

But in England, a Labour government was about to win a landslide election victory and usher in a new egalitarian age, and in Singapore too, the tide was slowly turning.

And now, having looked at a broad outline of the people and events that left their mark on the first sixty years of the Raffles's history, let us look at them compartmentalised, and in greater detail before going on to modern times and observing how the hotel faced and survived post-war crises.

5 ENTERTAINING THE GUESTS

A game of billiards was about all the entertainment you could expect at the Raffles Hotel in its early days. Occasionally, a circus would erect a big top on the reclaimed ground opposite the hotel, but the standard of the performances cannot have been very high if that put on by "Daddy" Abrams in 1897 is anything to go by. A press critic found it "a little monotonous", with its main attraction seeming to be "A procession of a score of horses moving round and round the field". Nevertheless, admission was free and the critic thought it "very good of Mr Abrams to afford such entertainment". As "Daddy" was an "equestrian supplier", his motivation may not have been quite as altruistic as it would appear on the surface.

For the most part in those pioneer days Singapore entertained itself, largely by means of amateur theatricals of highly variable quality. Their popularity derived mainly from their home-grown "stars", personal friends of almost everyone in the audience, and from numerous "in" jokes typical of a small, closed community.

There was uproar for instance at the doctoring of the Gilbert and Sullivan opera *The Yeomen of the Guard* in 1904 to include topical verses concocted by homespun local Cowards, who paid scant heed to scansion and whose wit was less than sparkling. Hard though it is to believe, this one, inserted into the traditional "Cock and Bull" duet, brought down a full house, packed with businessmen:

> "When exchange bobs up and down
> Then we hollar for a dollar that is fixed at half a crown.
> Or a shilling if you're willing.
> And they tell us every day
> We'll have fixity in this big city
> Before the month of May . . ."

The odd touring diva or actor from "Home" in Singapore en route to somewhere else, might condescend to give a one-night stand for benighted residents. (Many would say the situation has not vastly improved today, Singapore still being just an incidental stopover for world-class artistes.)

The "dancing years" of the 1920s and 1930s however saw a more settled community, relaxed on the economic, political and defence fronts, which could afford to pay for professional entertainment. The hotels became the centres for this new trend; by 1917 Raffles already had an orchestra playing nightly at dinner and at regular balls.

These years coincided with massive population movements in Europe after the

First World War, the Russian Revolution of 1917 and the consequent redrawing of boundaries and clanging of prison doors. Mine host at the Raffles, Arshak Sarkies, can hardly have ignored the fact that in 1915 the Ottoman Empire had decided to impose a "final solution" on its "Armenia question"—a solution that culminated in the massacre of an estimated one and a half million Christian Armenians, men, women and children, and an exodus of survivors who poured out in an Armenian equivalent of the Jewish diaspora.

As a result of all this turmoil, a horde of displaced persons, White Russian aristocrats, Poles, Slavs and Austrians, footed it overland, even across such terrifying terrain as Siberia, into Asia. The Russians in particular headed across the Siberian wastes for Harbin in Manchuria, just north of the Chinese border, thence making their way to that combination of romantic Shangri-La and cesspool that was Shanghai in the 1920s. Among these Russians were many finely schooled classical musicians, scions of a rejected intelligentsia, lumped unceremoniously by the revolutionaries into the same categories as the reviled ruling classes.

Such men were forced to make their living as best they could, and most were obliged to become jazz players in order to turn an honest penny. The new jazz music, fresh from America, was already pulsing through Shanghai by 1922. Hotels were the natural circuit for these itinerant musicians and so, from the Majestic in Shanghai, they would wend their way to the other great hotels of Asia—to the Grand in Calcutta, the Galle Face in Colombo, the Oriental in Bangkok, the Majestic in Kuala Lumpur, and, of course, to the Raffles in Singapore.

Typical of them was Joe Speelman, who was later to become manager of the old "Spotted Dog", as they call the Selangor Club in Kuala Lumpur, and a vice-president of the Kuala Lumpur Symphony Orchestra. He was a scared 17-year-old when he arrived in Shanghai from the Siberia-Harbin trek in 1921. He had grown up, the son of a Russian businessman, in St Petersburg, now Leningrad, where he studied the piano at six and gained admission to the famed St Petersburg Conservatory as a cello student at the age of nine. With his father killed in the First World War and the threat of the Russian Revolution driving them, he, with his mother and his cello, fled across Siberia to China, his mother setting up a restaurant in Harbin.

Joe was later to be one of the longest-staying musicians to grace the bandstand of the Raffles Hotel ballroom: "I was very comfortable and I didn't see any point to look for any other place. It was a funny sort of life", he mused in his seventies, Most people seem to have felt that way about the Raffles in those days, as they did too about Singapore—comfortable. Too comfortable, as later events were painfully to prove.

The first jazz band to play at the Raffles however was the Dan Hopkins Syncopated Five—or Quintette as it was later re-named. Dan Hopkins was a red headed Irish drummer who had originally been picked up by a Dixieland group in India in 1922, when he was company sergeant-major with a battalion of the

Cameron Highlanders, a regular soldier. The band, which was short of a drummer and desperate, finding that he was a dab-hand on the "skins", promptly "bought" him from his commanding officer for a mere £28.

The successors to Dan's outfit were Adeler and his Syncopators, who pulled out in 1925 after a one year's stint. The leader, South African-German pianist Edgar Adeler, with his banjoist partner, Al Bowlly, went to Surabaya, where they had a serious quarrel, which resulted in Bowlly's being left standing on the empty station platform, banjo and very little else in hand, while the train carrying Adeler and the rest of his band pulled out of town.

In Surabaya he met Dan Hopkins, who made him a loan. This, with savings he accumulated from a job in a cafe, was sufficient to enable him to sail to Calcutta. For a while this versatile man made a living as a jockey. Then he fell in with Jimmy Lequime, a fine alto sax player, who was destined subsequently to lead the Raffles orchestra in Singapore. The way in which jazz band players regularly disappeared and reappeared at the several fixed points on the hotel circuit in those days gives an idea of the close fraternity they had formed.

Joe Speelman had meanwhile found a job playing the cello in a Shanghai cinema, accompanying the silent films; but he was taking saxophone lessons in his spare time from Jimmy Lequime, who was then reigning supreme at Mumm House in Shanghai. He had another White Russian refugee in this band, pianist Monia Liter. An expanded version of Lequime's band were offered a long engagement at the Grand, Calcutta, so Lequime took with him Joe Speelman, who had by that time mastered the tenor sax. The other players were "Sax" MacGuire; Pete Harmon, another sax player who also specialised in "Al Jolson-style" singing; a Filipino, Nick Ampier, on the trombone; pianist Monia Liter; an American, Bill Houghton, drums; and an Austrian, Vic Halek, violin. Jimmy added the later famous singer Al Bowlly as banjoist and vocalist after the band's arrival in Calcutta. (But Bowlly's vocal style was then considered amusingly "sissy", which is why Harmon did most of the vocals at that stage.)

It was this band, minus Halek and Harmon, the latter replaced by charming but "wobbly" English sax player Eddie Beecher, that the Raffles hired from Calcutta in 1926.

From Calcutta to Singapore, the band exchanged audiences, jute planters for rubber planters—"After a few arranged numbers, the planters, who had plenty of money and drank prodigiously, would call for hotter music, and the fun would become fast and furious," Joe Speelman said.

Of the Lequime band he observed: "It was a happy band and when we were off-duty, we used to go everywhere together; we never quarrelled." They certainly needed each other's friendship, for there was very little chance of fraternising with the patrons of the Raffles—this apparently was "not done".

Still, the wild men from Shanghai (some of whom kept a convenient bottle of booze under their chairs while performing, to allay the *ennui* natural to such fine musicians during such mundane chores) did manage to jazz up the customers' lives a bit. Joe Speelman says he was the first man to do the Charleston in the

Raffles, instantly acquiring a number of eager pupils. The Charleston remained "slightly shocking" until surprisingly late, according to several other musicians playing at the time.

Joe Speelman liked what he saw in Singapore: "It was an exotic place, very colonial and very cultural. The existing musicians were mainly Goanese who performed much for the silent films in those days. When sound tracks came with the films, these Goanese moved into the cabarets and dance music. They were very good musicians and some of their children are still top musicians in Singapore and Malaysia today," he recalled. These Goanese would have been mainly Portuguese or Portuguese-Eurasians, who then played much the same dominant role in Asian musical circles as Filipinos do now.

At first, the Lequime band's music must have been much as Joe Speelman described it in Calcutta, with Sax MacGuire wandering among the diners with his "C" Melody sax for the more sentimental numbers. A recording made just before the band sailed for Singapore and the Raffles, at HMV Dum Dum Studios, Calcutta, has preserved for posterity "The House Where the Shutters are Green", a Monia Liter composition, and "Soho Blues", the words for both songs

Jimmy Lequime's Band.
Taken at Calcutta Zoo 1926 during their stint at the Grand Hotel, Calcutta. Left to right—"Sax" Macguire, Pete Harmon, Al Bowlly, Nick Amper and Vic Halek.
By courtesy of Henry Stonor and Joe Speelman

Jimmy Lequime's Band, c. December 1926 at Raffles. Left to right, back: Jack Lippe (drums), Al Bowlly; front: "Sax" Macguire (saxes), Monia Liter (piano), Jimmy Lequime (trumpet), Eddie Beecher (saxes) and Joe Speelman (saxes). By courtesy of Henry Stonor and Joe Speelman

being written by Pete Harmon. Roberto Pregarz, manager of the Raffles at the time of writing this book, possesses a taped copy of this.

Friendly though it may have been, the Lequime band began to disintegrate soon after its arrival in Singapore, with the departure first of Lequime himself to become a businessman, then of Bill Houghton, bound for South Africa, and of Al Bowlly in 1927, amazingly enough to join his "friend" Edgar Adeler (the one who had abandoned him at Surabaya station) in Germany. Al was later discovered down and out, busking on London's street corners, in 1929. "Al Bowlly was a bum", was Dan Hopkins' caustic comment on his old band-mate, in 1972.

Sax MacGuire took over the band leadership from Lequime; but, after the departure of Nick Ampier for Shanghai, and of Eddie Beecher, the wobbly saxophonist, Sax himself left in 1928, with only one kidney, pickled in alcohol at that. Disregarding the doctor's injunction to go teetotal, Sax died soon after

The Raffles Today

The Palm Court – Interior

The Palm Court – Exterior

The Tiffin Room

RAFFLES HOTEL

SARKIES BROS, Proprietors

FINE CHAMPAGNE
MARIE BRIZARD & ROGER
COGNAC

Modèle déposé. Imp. P. Vercasson & Cⁱᵉ, Paris.

Undated postcards from the Sarkies family collection – probably turn of the century. Note the rickshaws and tram outside the hotel

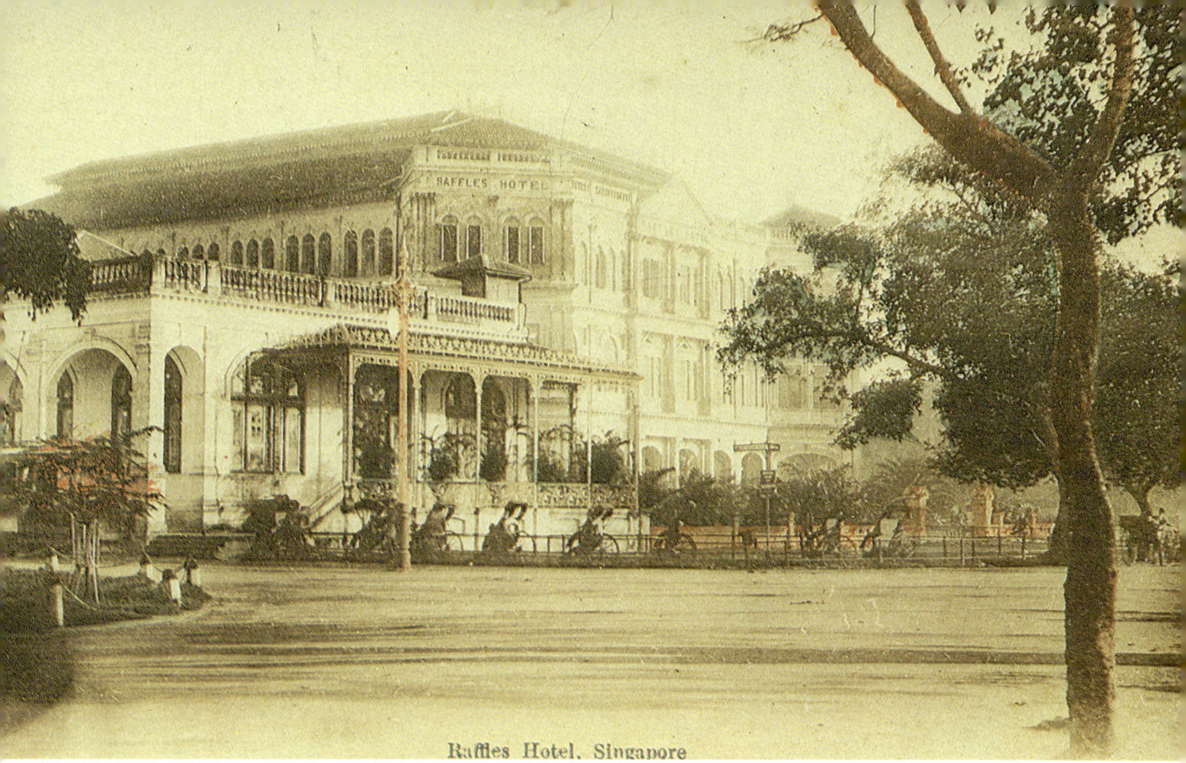

Raffles Hotel, Singapore

Raffles mementoes —
the old front entrance
and the P & O
wharf

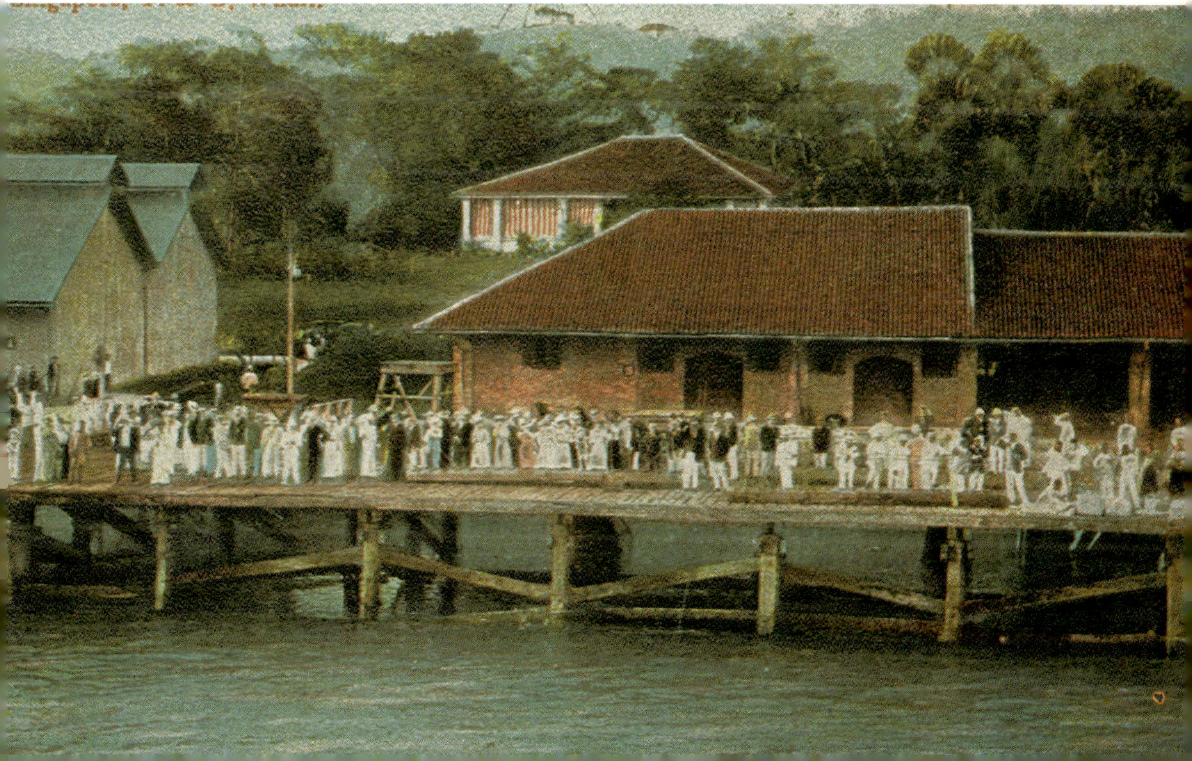

Food at the Raffles

Above: Curry Tiffin

Left: Buffet in the Palm Court – photograph by John Hedgcoe

Below: Sucking Pig

apore Sling

Bok Siang Han in the kitchen

Margarine sculpture

Raffles front door

reaching California, with a Singapore souvenir, malaria, complicating his careless indulgence in the bottle.

By 1929, of the original Lequime band only Monia Liter, now band-leader, and Joe Speelman still remained in the Raffles. Many circles were completed when Dan Hopkins returned from London to join them at the end of 1928. Arshak Sarkies, holidaying in England, had walked into the Savoy in London and spotted Dan playing there. At his invitation, Dan sailed for Singapore to beef up Monia Liter's now rather tired version of Lequime's team. More White Russians—most with classical training, who lived for Sunday nights, when they could perform as a classical orchestra—were hired, but, according to planter Henry Stonor, "the band was somewhat lifeless", despite Monia's "hot" piano and Dan's inspired drumming.

Dan Hopkins took over the band again when Monia Liter left in 1931 after a "difference of opinion" with the Raffles management over casual leave. Monia sailed for England—where both he and Al Bowlly eventually won fame, Al as

Dan Hopkins' Band, 1933, at Raffles.
Left to right, back: Bob Kauff, Dan Hopkins, Enrico Dallio: centre: Unidentified (?) Jan Kleinman, Carl Marrachek, Trevor Mays; front, alone: Buster Johnson.
By courtesy of Henry Stonor and Joe Speelman

"The Man with the Velvet Voice" (his style was no longer considered "sissy" now that the raucous Al Jolson vogue had waned), and Monia as a British Broadcasting Corporation arranger. Apparently business came before sentiment with the hotel management, just in transition at this point from the late generous Arshak Sarkies' wayward *modus operandi* to a more impersonal, "modern" approach, overshadowed by the Sarkies' recent bankruptcy and some very shaky account books. Oblivious to the musical treasures in which the Raffles ballroom was rejoicing, the management decreed that Monia, and anyone else who did not work his contract to the last letter, would have to go.

Al Bowlly was killed in his flat by a bomb during a wartime air raid on London; Monia, at the time of writing, was still alive and at the piano in London. On his departure, Monia was replaced at the Raffles by an Australian pianist, Abe Walters, whose trumpeter brother, Wally, also joined the band, together with Don Binney on the trombone. Now only the faithful Joe Speelman remained of Lequime's original band. An old Shanghai hand, lanky Bob Kauff, a Russian nicknamed "Boris Karloff" for his lowering looks, took over on string and brass bass in 1932, and after a couple more switches at the piano, Dodo Mailinger, a Hungarian, settled in at the keyboard.

The 1932-33 season benefited from the appearance in the band of a jazz personality, Buster Johnson, trombonist composer of the "Wang Wang Blues", recorded in 1945 with Paul Whiteman on Capitol's "History of Jazz" series.

Dan Hopkins (left) with Wally Walters (right), 1933, in Raffles' Palm Court. By courtesy of Heny Stonor and Joe Speelman

Hopkins recalled in 1972: "Buster went Japanese—eating Japanese food, wearing Japanese clothes and living in a Japanese furnished house."

Another population upheaval, like the Armenian exodus, began as Hitler's Germany began to show its real face, and so in 1936 Otto Joaquim of the alto and baritone saxophone (whose name suggests he may have been an Armenian, but possibly he was a Jew), fled Germany and joined the Raffles band, making the 1938 line-up: Dan Hopkins (drums); Joe Speelman (alto and baritone sax); Otto Joaquim (ditto); New Zealander Maurice Gilman (clarinet and tenor sax); Wally Walters (trumpet); Dodo Mailinger (piano), and Bob Kauff (string bass and sousaphone).

This was the band which played bravely on as the Japanese advanced on Singapore in 1942, give or take a few members—Walters and Gilman were replaced just before the fall of Singapore by Jimmy Sullivan on trumpet and Danny Danford, sax and vocal, both Americans, and Gerry Soliano, Filipino, joined the sax section. Soliano says there were also Conrad Gregorio on the tenor sax and Harry Levine, "a beautiful poker player".

Gerry Soliano had arrived in Singapore in 1922, having played in a Medan cinema while his father was on contract to the Dutch East Indies government. He played first at a couple of cinemas, then at the Sarkies' Sea View Hotel in Singapore's Katong district. The Raffles Hotel band would play on Tuesdays and Fridays at the Sea View, Wednesdays and Saturdays at the Raffles.

The Raffles band's monopoly of the Singapore cabaret scene however faced its first serious challenge in 1940 when "Innocent Nick"—Niconishen Markovitch Innokenty, another St Petersburg Conservatory cello graduate—brought his "Hot Six" to the Tanglin Club as resident band, a worthy rival for Dan Hopkins and his merry men.

Many have been the descriptions, in the best purple prose, of the evening scene at the Raffles in the immediate pre-war period. They all paint the same picture of the patrons—most of them expatriate Englishmen and their wives or mistresses—arriving in sleek cars, the doors of which are opened by an expressionless turbaned doorman. His ministrations are taken over by an equally obsequious cloakroom attendant before the couples make their way to tables set under palm trees whose barely moving foliage hides only portions of a sky studded with brilliant stars.

The guests intersperse consumption of the tempting dishes on the *haute cuisine* menu and wines from a formidable list of the choicest vintages with sallies to the ballroom floor behind the Palm Court. For the most part they take their pleasures sadly—or at least stiffly and unemotionally—in the traditional British manner, showing signs of animation only when Danny waves his baton to start a jitterbug measure.

As ever, the servants stand around with impassive faces, commenting to each other, *sotto voce*, on the immorality of the European women who show themselves in public places with their arms, shoulders and backs bare, and allow

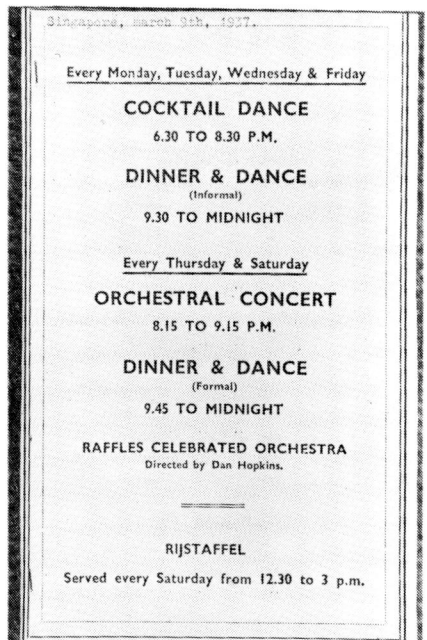

Advertisement.
By courtesy of Ray Tyers and Raffles Hotel

themselves to be taken in this state of near nudity into the arms of their partners, and then indulge in indecorous, coupled gyrations on the dance floor.

Many of the biggest "bashes", as these revelries were known to the habitués, were organised on such true-blue British occasions as St George's, St Andrew's or St David's day. They ended with a firm reminder of colonial status, "God save the King", or, as the Second World War got closer, a desperate "There'll always be an England".

It must have been an essay in boredom for the hot-blooded Russians and Hungarians, and easygoing, democratic-minded Americans playing in Dan's band, perched on the ballroom dais like dummies in what Soliano described as "long trousers clipped in at the ankle", trying to enliven similar dummies on the dance floor. Small wonder many of them were driven to drink. The colour scheme alone must have been somewhat nauseous, for colour flooding had been installed in 1934, as well as a soft grey ceiling and green railings for the ballroom, the floor of which was constructed of brown glass "boards".

And it must have been doubly hard for those virtuoso Russian classicists to churn out "If you knew Suzie . . ." or "Bye Bye Blackbird", as they did, especially on Services Night, Wednesday. Fortunately a military band relieved them on Sunday evenings, and apparently pulled in the troops in big numbers.

Music was not the only entertainment in the Raffles in those days, although it certainly dominated. One of the longest-term entertainers of all at Raffles was Doris Mabel Geddes, née Henderson, Sydney-born in 1904, a former stage pianist and dancer, who, as we have seen, later took over a boutique in the hotel's shopping arcade.

The Australian immigration men told Doris she couldn't go to dance in Shanghai unless she had a return ticket—they wanted to protect the tender 22-year-old from the "sinful East". Returning from Shanghai, she landed up on the India circuit, via Indonesia, and in 1929 married Len Geddes, chairman of Wearne Brothers in Singapore, after meeting him in Burma and again on the same ship sailing from Rangoon to Singapore.

Piles of yellowing scrapbooks reveal her to have been one of the brightest lights on the glittering social scene at the Raffles of the 1930s, when she spent her time largely in organising charity variety shows and fashion parade extravaganzas; the "Pageant of Youth and Beauty" for example, in which eligible local misses paraded as characters such as Marie Antionette and La Pompadour. "Doris's gels" were legend among the young bachelors, eagerly sought-after dancing partners—particularly two striking Eurasian lovelies, Rachel and Rosa Sum, daughters of an Indonesian millionaire—and were among the very select few Asians allowed to dance freely on the Raffles ballroom floor without too many eyebrows raised.

A dance turn by a couple known as "Kira and Boris" was performed in the ballroom three times weekly in early 1936. The male partner, Boris Lissanevitch, a Russian ballet dancer who danced with Nijinsky, is now a legend in Nepal, his one-time Yak and Yeti hostelry having figured prominently in novelist Han Suyin's *The Mountain is Young*. Kira was his wife. They did classical and character dancing or "Comedy dances from *The Gay Nineties* and that sort of thing," according to Boris.

His 1936 stint was his second at the Raffles—he had also performed there in 1934 ("I had been on a three months' shooting trip to Laos and Vietnam, so I thought I might as well see the East,") before setting up Calcutta's first multiracial club, the famous 300, where he had first displayed his fabled talents as hotelier and restaurateur par excellence.

The 300 Club had been yet another venue for many a wandering jazzman, Joe Speelman for one. Moving in the gilded circles he did, it was hardly surprising that Boris too should make a beeline for the Raffles, a "must" on the colonial circuit.

Having left Russia in 1924, as a refugee, Boris was obliged to travel on the infamous Nansen passport for stateless persons—"a terrible document to travel with—we were not wanted"—and managed to move freely in and out of countries like Singapore thanks only to his friendship with Lady Diana Duff Cooper, actress wife of the Rt. Hon. Alfred Duff Cooper, Member of the British House of Commons and later Lord Norwich. She would "cable the Governor and fix it for me".

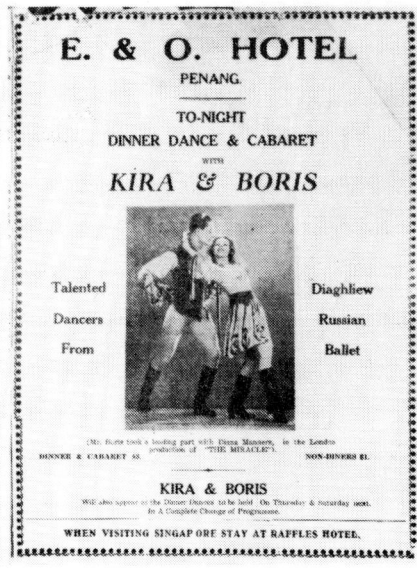

Newspaper advertisement of the 1930's for the Kira and Boris duo (Boris Lissanevitch, now of Kathmandu, and his wife) at the E and O hotel, an act which also played at the Raffles.
By courtesy of Boris Lissanevitch

Cooper arrived in Singapore in 1941 at the behest of the British War Cabinet, and at the outbreak of the Pacific War was appointed Resident Minister for Far Eastern Affairs with Cabinet rank. He headed the Far East War Council, comprising Sir Shenton Thomas, Singapore's Governor, Lt. General Arthur Percival, General Officer Commanding in Malaya, and other war leaders.

Throughout the late 1930s the competition from the Tanglin Club was beginning to bite, and not just because of Innocent Nick's "Hot Six". The cause was the restrictive licensing hours imposed on hotels but not on clubs. In 1937 the Chairman's report to the annual general meeting of the hotel attributed its $13,766 loss partly to competition from clubs, complaining that Hongkong was far more liberal with its licensing hours. The hotel, he said, had recently been forced to turn away good business in the shape of a liner in port with 500 passengers, for want of extended licensing hours.

This really hurt, for world unrest at the time meant that the tourist pickings were getting more and more sparse, the only liners in port usually being Royal Navy combat and patrol vessels.

To add to the Raffles's woes, entertainment tax was introduced in 1940; the hotel management manfully pledged it would not raise its dance prices however, although it cost only about $10 a head for dinner with cabaret at that time.

During the Japanese occupation, Appelbaum's Hungarian band, which had been marooned at the Adelphi Hotel when the enemy arrived, played at the Raffles. They rendered a mixture of classical Western music and Japanese favourites—a laxity which must have been permitted only for the very senior Japanese officers staying at the Raffles then, since the Japanese in Malaya generally banned all Western music. The Raffles staff must have missed the familiar foxtrots, tangos and seductive saxophones of their colonial masters; and the Hungarians must have found it a mite hard to mimic alien Japanese jingles.

But somehow things were never the same again in the Raffles ballroom. After the Japanese surrender in 1945, the hotel could not afford a band, but offered free accommodation to any group which would play and help get things swinging again.

Good old Joe Speelman, last of the Lequime band, was first into the hotel after the war, even putting in a couple of months' stint as temporary assistant manager, so short-staffed was the hotel. He formed a new band with Dodo Mailinger and Bob Kauff, both pre-war performers at the Raffles, as well as Aussie newcomers Tenber and Taylor on trumpet and alto sax; Tibor Kunstler, a Hungarian, on tenor sax; Martin, a Filipino, on drums; and an Australian singer, Joan Frazer.

Dan Hopkins meanwhile was also back in Singapore with a servicemen's band at the Victoria Hall. But in 1948 Speelman's boys disbanded, having given a farewell classical concert. Hopkins too was soon to close shop and join Radio Malaya.

The dance-band era was drawing to its close throughout the world, and, as Speelman said, "Singapore after the war was restless, like the rest of the world". The growing attractions of cinema, as well as rival dance halls, coupled with the

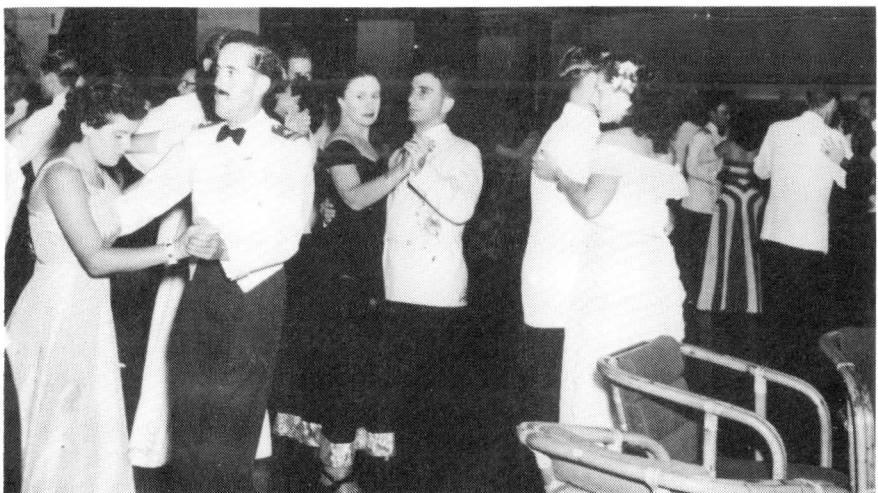

Ballroom Gala Opening, May 1st 1948, in Raffles. Note the white evening jackets for the tropics, mess jackets etc.
By courtesy of *Straits Times*

newly unfashionable colonialist connotations of even being seen at the Raffles, amounted to a thumbs down for Raffles' night-life.

Speelman went on to manage the Griffin Inn Club in Kuala Lumpur, then the Orchid Hotel in Johor Baru, and still later Kuala Lumpur's Selangor Club.

Dan Hopkins was dug out of his ramshackle Singapore flat by planter Henry Stonor in 1972, a lonely and reclusive old man, clad only in baggy Chinese shorts, suspicious of and hostile to would-be visitors. He died in 1973.

Poor Dodo Mailinger suffered a severe stroke in his old age and spent his last days at the Singapore Cheshire Home for the permanently handicapped and disabled.

Gerry Soliano's Raffles Orchestra was through most of the 1950s the resident band, supplemented by visitors such as Alice Lee, "Nightingale of the Orient", and that greatest, perhaps, of South American rhythm exponents, Xavier Cugat and his Nugats, besides dance acts such as Les Kirdalls, Anita and Armand and Bettine, "modern dancer"; singers such as "lyric" sopranos Tina Laine and Sylvia Gareh and baritones Paterson Hutton and Montgomery Robinson.

The Raffles Manager Frans Schutzman (left) with entertainer Xavier Cugat, at the hotel in 1953.
By courtesy of Frans Schutzman and the Raffles

In the mid-1950s, the Raffles was the first local hotel to acquire a Hammond organ, and Gerry Soliano claimed to have been the first Malayan to play one.

The 1950s also saw the Raffles pulling off a promotional coup: relayed music from the hotel's ballroom was broadcast over local radio for half an hour every Thursday night at 10.30 pm, often with popular local vocalists, Poppy and Margie Manasseh, or Rosalie and Freddy Jansen (the former were Jewish-Singaporean, the latter Singapore Eurasians), and compèred by Singapore Eurasian Vernon Palmer, who at the time of writing is Assistant Director (Training) at the Singapore Broadcasting Corporation.

But a new era was dawning and even music was not immune from politics, particularly when it sheltered beneath the roof of an arch-colonial symbol like the Raffles. This was a time of racial and political riots, worker protests and trade union activism, with the Malayan guerrilla war in full swing on the mainland. Singapore was heading for crucial elections offering partial self-government in 1955, and full independence in 1959.

The Singapore Musicians' Union was probably influenced by its secretary, later president, Gerry Soliano, who, as a Singaporean and in any case Filipino-born, was an acceptable Asian leader, when it decided to hold its gala annual ball at the Raffles in December 1951.

An advertisement from the 1950s. By courtesy of the Raffles

Cabaret with Gerry Soliano at Raffles Hotel in the 1950s. Soliano on violin (left).
The Manasseh sisters (right) with orchestra leader Gerry Soliano.
By courtesy of Gerry Soliano, taken by Peter Robinson Studios, Singapore

Ironically, however, Raffles was also one of the hotels marked out for union censure in the following months when the union protested against the general practice of using imported foreign bands at local hotels. The Raffles, along with other hotels, was obliged to agree that it should always at least match each foreign band hired with a local one. Grumbling, the management noted sourly at the 1950 annual general meeting that the replacement of its former orchestra with a local one had been "not satisfactory".

This trend however accelerated with the years. In 1957, with Chief Minister Lim Yew Hock operating an uneasy transitional Government under the wing of the British colonial authorities, pending negotiation of complete self-government, it was natural that the authorities should be anxious to appear as nationalist as possible, if only to contain the gathering forces threatening to tear Singapore apart.

At this point then, the immigration authorities ruled that only two foreign bands could play in the entire colony at any one time, and that no hotel could employ such a band for more than six months at a time.

Gone were the days when Lady Duff Cooper could get the Governor to "fix it"; gone were the days when rag-tag refugees could troop across borders at random, the world their oyster. All the world was not a single stage.

The Raffles promptly closed its ballroom down and the Dutch manager, Frans Schutzman, angrily challenged the local musicians' union to find a good local band "that can keep people interested".

The hotel was to complain even more loudly in 1959 against "what amounts to a ban on the procurement of a really high-class orchestra", after the election of Singapore's first independent and, at that time, strongly anti-colonial government formed by the People's Action Party, which still rules today.

It was perhaps not entirely coincidental that during the late 1950s the Raffles board included not only colonials but locals such as conservative Baba (Straits-born Chinese) banker and politician Tan Chin Tuan, who was active in the pro-colonial Progressive Party. This party was to be bypassed by more impatient, radical nationalists like Lee Kuan Yew, who has led the People's Action Party government as Prime Minister since 1959. Ironically, the two men are, related by marriage. Mr Tan, chairman of the Raffles board in 1959, is now chairman of the Oversea-Chinese Banking Corporation, which is the majority share-holder and operating company of the Raffles.

Yet another indication of changing times was the fact that "Malayan Night" floorshows, featuring traditional Malay dances and rituals, were first mooted in 1956, sign of the growing belief that Singapore's future lay in a merger with Malaya. These shows are still on the programme at Raffles today, though separation in 1965 shattered the merger dream.

6 BEHIND THE SCENES: THE MANAGERS

For many years, the Sarkies were the Raffles, and vice versa. Their personal touch and strong personalities made the hotel the fashionable venue that it was during the 1920s and 1930s. But as the venture grew, probably even beyond their own wildest expectations, and as they themselves aged, they had to call upon others to assist them—and invariably those others were, in the early days at least, fellow Armenians.

A single, one-line reference suggests there may have been an Armenian manager at the Raffles in the 1890s, named Joaquim, but the best known of the Sarkies right-hand men was undoubtedly Joseph ("Joe") Constantine, also an Armenian, who worked as the "chief" at Raffles from the beginning and later moved to their new venture, the Strand in Rangoon. A writer in the 1920s said Joe "passed thousands of passengers through his hands with unfailing urbanity".

The phenomenon of a hired, professional hotel manager, an outsider who was not also one of the hotel owners, however, barely occurred until the Raffles passed from the hands of the Sarkies to a more impersonal public company, following the family company bankruptcy in 1931.

The last Armenian manager ("He had that big Armenian nose" say hotel staff who remember him) was Martyrose Sarkies Arathoon, also a partner in the company from 1916 onwards, an experienced but unqualified accountant who joined the brothers as secretary to the Raffles in 1905, leaving his job with a Manchester piece goods firm. (Men with such jobs were often the butt of snobbish remarks and jokes among the European colonials in Singapore, for "the Manchester piece goods man" was considered the epitome of vulgarity. With such "image" problems, it is doubtful whether Arathoon ever won the popularity that the Sarkies enjoyed and he was probably socially relegated to the company of Eurasians, Sindis and Parsis.)

Arathoon found himself in full charge long before 1916, while the older Sarkies brothers travelled and Arshak based himself at the E and O in Penang. After Tigran's retirement and death in 1917, and his brother Aviet's death in 1923, Arathoon was well established in control. His relationship with Arshak, however, deteriorated steadily as he, a wizard at figures, capable of adding up stacked columns of figures at one glance, began to realise that all was not well with Arshak's management of the books, particularly in his "home territory", Penang.

Arshak, prey to the family weakness for betting on "the gee-gees", and full of grandiose plans for expensive expansion of the E and O, depression or no depression, resented Arathoon's advice as "interference" and an "insult", but, said Arathoon in court later, they were on bad terms "only from a business point of view". Unfortunately, the pair of them were also constantly at loggerheads with the other dead Sarkies brothers' families about their shares in the business.

Arathoon was the unlucky sole survivor of the Sarkies brothers' company after Arshak's death in January 1931, and by August, he was taking the rap in the Singapore bankruptcy court for Arshak's follies, aggravated by the general slump of that time. At the age of 61, he was thus an unwilling protagonist in the final collapse of the Sarkies concern, amid unseemly bickering among the partners' widows. He himself was roundly accused by Arshak's widow of leaving her without a penny.

Arathoon and his son, Sarkies Martyrose Arathoon, were, however, kept on at the hotel by the new company. Perhaps this was a measure of their indispensability, or more likely, of the chaotic complexity of the hotel's books which only they could unravel. They were retained although the bankruptcy court had discharged Arathoon on the condition that he have no further stake in any hotel business. But his hour was to come again when the Japanese interned all Europeans during their occupation of Singapore, and he was left to act as sole local manager of Raffles for the duration.

Arathoon is remembered by Quek Chua Koon, one of the cashiers, who joined the hotel as an 18-year-old in 1946, as "a very nice man, very kind, and very good at figures. He always had a nap at 3.00 pm and he would twiddle his thumbs whenever he was facing problems".

But a franker assessment of the Sarkies and Arathoons probably comes from chief cashier Tan Geok Swee, who retired in 1980 as chief cashier having worked at the hotel since 1936. He says, "The Armenians were very difficult, hard taskmasters. They taught me to be very persevering and tolerant."

Arathoon senior, poor fellow, must have done more than his share of anxious thumb-twiddling before he died at the ripe old age of 84, having run for some time his own general trading company, Arathoon and Sons, in Battery Road. For, apart from his own appearance in court, he was to live to see his 46-year-old son, Sarkies, who was appointed chief accountant in 1946 and often worked as assistant manager too, sentenced to two years' imprisonment in 1949 for criminal breach of trust involving no less than $88,930 of the hotel's money. The judge said he had perpetrated "systematic fraud" over more than a year, making false entries in the hotel books by omitting the odd zero here and there. Sarkies said he had "lost" the money, but had no further defence. His downfall, needless to say, had been the horse-races. He died in 1981 in an old people's home.

Such was the sad end to the Armenian stake in the hotel.

The man hired as manager by the new company, to supervise the sorry mess that the Raffles had now become, was a Swiss, a professional hotelier. Theodore ("Teddy") Troller was 42 when he arrived to take up his post in 1933.

Like the musicians who played at the hotel during his time, he too had travelled the "Shanghai route" that was almost mandatory then for service in the Far East. From 1923–1927 he had been responsible for the Majestic and Astor House hotels in Shanghai, and had served as manager at the Grand Hotel Wagons Lits, Peking. Even at that point, he already had considerable experience behind him in

Europe, especially in England—at the Piccadilly and Regent Palace in London, at the Trocadero Restaurant, the Majestic in St Annes and the Queen's in Cheltenham, and as general manager of Lyons Ltd—as well as at the Ritz Carlton in New York.

Only a sketchy portrait of Troller is possible. Staff say that he was "strict", and certainly his photos suggest a somewhat icy, probably authoritarian character. "His attitude was that 'work is work'," comments one of his staff, a big change from the Armenian flamboyance of the Sarkies.

Troller's 49-year-old wife, Annie, died towards the end of 1939 and after this, he took a year's leave of absence in Europe, leaving his assistant manager, an Italian named Guido Cevenini, in charge of the hotel.

All we know of the remaining period before the Japanese occupation in 1942 is that by the time the invaders arrived in Singapore Troller had already left for Durban in South Africa. It was, however, during Troller's time that the hotel was finally dragged into the twentieth century, with large-scale physical changes, such as the installation of modern bathrooms and sanitation, taking place.

Guido Cevenini, who, after the war at least, seems to have alternated as manager with his brother Nino whenever it suited him, was the first link in Raffles's long-standing "Italian connection", which has been responsible for the sequence of fine Italian dishes that still feature prominently on the Raffles menu today, for the unusual number of Italian guests, and for loyal patronage from the Italian embassy and the Italian airline, Alitalia.

Every inch the stereotype Italian—"hotblooded", said Frans Schutzman, a later manager—Guido was colourful, considered a "handsome devil" to boot, generous and ever so slightly wild. This must have seemed to the staff a nostalgic reminder of the good old days with Arshak Sarkies.

Schutzman recalls that Cevenini was the kind of man who, when a Foreign Legionnaire chose the Raffles as his base for jumping ship in Singapore, "bailed him out of jail and made him head-waiter, just because he felt sorry for him. But he was a useless waiter"! True to his temperamental type, however, Cevenini was just as ready to tell Schutzman that he could have that very waiter's job at the drop of a hat—"I'll give him a month's notice and you can be *maitre d'* in the dining room", he said. Obviously, the Raffles management was not yet quite the impersonal, efficiently modern concern that the owners might have preferred.

Guido had hotels in his blood, however; he was born into a family of hoteliers from Bologna, also his wife's home-town. He proved his loyalty to the Raffles later when he made a beeline back to the hotel in 1946, to take it over from the by then ailing Arathoons, after having been interned in Australia as an enemy national for five years.

At Cevinini's side in 1946 was Ernest Smith, the English assistant manager who had served at the Raffles since the age of 24 in 1938, with both Troller and himself. Smith, another Swiss-trained hotelier, described Cevenini as "my very good friend", and we have seen the strength of that friendship in his guardianship of the Cevenini jewels through the war.

Teddy Troller
Manager of Raffles, and first professional to succeed the Sarkies family management in the 1930s under the new Raffles Hotel company.
By courtesy of the *Straits Times*

Guido Cevenini and wife Marisa, April 17, 1952.
The *Straits Times* report reads: "Mr Guido Cevenini, general manager of Raffles Hotel, greeted his bride of seven months, Marisa, when she arrived in Singapore yesterday, on board the Italian liner *Sebastiano Caboto*. First gift from husband is—you've guessed—Suzie, a two and a half months' old cocker spaniel."
By courtesy of the *Straits Times*

The Cevenini management style, he said, was more democratic, something of a novelty in those days. "In the old days, it was 'Boy!' to call the staff, but at least we called them 'Tan' or 'Ong'".

But the much loved Guido ("very understanding and noble-minded" say the staff) suffered a stroke which paralysed him in late 1952, while Smith was on long home leave in England. Naturally, Guido had to be sent home to Italy, where he later died. It was tough luck for Smith that at this crucial juncture the ambitious and forceful Frans Schutzman was hovering in the wings, waiting for his cue. He seized it with alacrity.

A Dutchman born in Surabaya, in 1915, Schutzman had arrived in Malaya in 1952, shortly before Cevenini's heart attack, as a free-lance journalist, serving mainly Scandinavian papers. He wanted to write on the emergency then under way in Malaya, and on the flamboyant President Sukarno's regime in Indonesia.

Ernest Smith, assistant manager (left) with HJCK Toms, chairman, Straits Steamship company, at Straits Steamship 60th anniversary function, Raffles, January 1950.
By courtesy of Ray Tyers

"I was discreetly informed that, if I continued to Jakarta, I would be arrested as a spy", he says with a grin.

Stranded and with only $10 in his pocket, Schutzman drew on his undeniable charm and initiative and went to see Cevenini at the Raffles, asking for a job. No job, said Cevenini flatly. "I said I would wash dishes, anything", Schutzman recalls, "but he told me, 'You can't do that! It's a colonial government here, you know—they won't let a European wash dishes!'"

Desperate, Schutzman resorted to shock tactics: "I told him that when I had walked into his so-called 'world-famous' hotel, the receptionist had been sitting on a chair, and when I walked past the ballroom, I saw waiters in dirty uniforms, their fingers up their noses, scratching and so on. I had asked myself, was this really the famous Raffles Hotel?"

Cevenini got mad, which was what I wanted. He said, "Did you come here for a job, or to insult the management of the Raffles Hotel?" "Don't you have anyone to help you?" I asked. "Yes," he said, "I do".

It was at this point that Cevenini offered to sack the unfortunate former Foreign Legionnaire but, said the dogged Schutzman, "I cannot wait a month." Cevenini, characteristically generous, first lectured him, telling him he was crazy to come to Singapore without money or a job, then told him to go to a boarding house run by some friends of his, where he would personally cover his bill.

Three days later, Cevenini had got rid of the wretched waiter and Schutzman had the job. At his first function, a St George's Day dinner, he was confronted with a sizeable hunk of Ye Olde English roast beef to be carved at table for none other than the Governor of Singapore, Sir Franklin Gimson.

"Mr Cevenini", said Schutzman, trembling with apprehension, "I have never sliced roast beef in my life. I am scared to death." Cevenini sent him off to the bar forthwith for a stiff double brandy and, declares Schutzman, "By God, I was the greatest roast beef-slicer ever that night!"

It was the beginning of a life-time career for a distinguished, and self-taught, hotelier, who was at heart an adventurer, one might even say a buccaneer. He was to show his more piratical side six months later when Cevenini was taken ill.

Smith declined to cut short his vacation in England at this point, as he was already considering another job offer from Australia, and so the board decided to appoint Schutzman joint manager with Smith, since he was the only other

Frans Schutzman (centre) serving the Governor 'Ye Old English Roast Beef' during a St George's Dinner in the 1950s, while working as Maitre d'Hotel. By courtesy of Frans Schutzman and the Raffles Hotel; taken by the Raffles photographers

easily available European. But Schutzman politely demurred, suggesting that Smith should be manager, himself assistant manager.

Asked to leave the room, he was recalled after a few minutes' deliberation by the board, to be told: "OK, you're the manager, Smith your assistant manager."

But the shameless Schutzman, not content, asked for more. Why not let him be sole manager? The board bowed to his ambition. Smith and the hotel parted company at this point: he secured a Sheffield silverware representation while in England and the by now magnanimous Schutzman promptly ordered all the Raffles' silverware from him.

Schutzman, who does not count humility among his many virtues, now comments, "I am glad to say Smith is today a very prosperous businessman, and much happier than as a hotelier." Smith, now a Singaporean by passport, does indeed run his own business partnership, Dyer and Smith, a combination trading and tour promotion firm, as well as a highly successful tourism venture, the Villa Saujana at the picturesque seaside village of Loyang in Singapore, where visitors spill out by the coach-load to gorge on good local curry *makan* and goggle at Malay cultural shows.

Schutzman meanwhile proceeded to imprint his gargantuan personality on the Raffles, which, as he is the first to point out, paid out a 25 percent dividend to shareholders for the first time ever just 18 months after his installation as manager.

He has since done similarly sterling service at the Nile Hilton in Cairo, the Hotel Cavalieri Hilton in Rome, the Hyatt Regency in Toronto and the UN Plaza in New York and is now ensconced at the gracious old Manila in the Philippines, where he is in his element once more with the old world charm that the Manila shares with the Raffles.

But all the luxuries of the famous hostelries with which he has been connected are as nothing in comparison with Frans Schutzman's "dream hotel". "I want a 20-suite hotel on the French Riviera," he once told the catering industry magazine *Hospitality*. "The most exclusive, the most beautiful. It will be only for my millionaire friends and will cost $1,000 a day. They will have at their disposal a Rolls-Royce and a chauffeur; the greatest chef in the world will cook for them; they will have the best vintage wines, the most exclusive artistes like Sammy Davis Jr and Frank Sinatra just for them. A yacht will be at their disposal and they will eat and drink as much as they like."

Even though the Raffles has long since passed from his suzerainty, he, typically, still has firm ideas on what to do with the Raffles today: "I would build a 600-room tower behind it—leave the Palm Court and take that horrid spittoon of a swimming pool out, plant orchids, put coloured parrots, make it tropical."

The son of a Dutch watch-maker based in Java, Schutzman had already been a music publisher before he turned to his short-lived career as a journalist. Later he was to add "spy" to his exotic *curriculum vitae*, for he was active in British intelligence during the war.

Rarely diplomatic, he once told an enraged guest complaining that an inch-long worm had crawled out of his salad just as he was about to "pop the question" to his beloved: "I was once married myself, and thinking back on all the aggravations and the money it cost me to get a divorce, I wish a rattlesnake had come out of *my* salad when I decided to declare myself to my ex-wife."

That "people make hotels" is axiomatic in Frans Schutzman's view, and he expects his executives to eat regularly with their rank-and-file hotel staff. He says one of his principal departures as manager of the Raffles was to feed the staff: "They had quarters behind the hotel, but no food, so logically of course, they had to steal food. I decided to feed them when I discovered this. Why, all they needed was the fish-heads we chucked out (fish-head is a Singaporean gourmet delicacy), some rice and vegetables!"

"The hotel management put me on the carpet. 'Who authorised you to feed them?' I was asked. I replied, 'You should first ask me how it is we are making so much money now? I'll tell you why, because the staff are not eating up our expensive ham and roast beef any more, that's why! I feed them cheap food—hence our total food costs are lower.'"

Steadfast defender of "class" that he is, Schutzman once opined: "There's one way *not* to build business and that is by substantially lowering room rates. Giving away rooms at half price will eventually lower the standards of a hotel."

Thanks to the Raffles, Schutzman was to count such luminaries as the Sultan of Johor, Ava Gardner, Gloria Swanson and other distinguished guests at the hotel, among his closest friends.

It was Schutzman who first spotted the famous reference by Somerset Maugham to the Raffles as standing for "all the fables of the exotic East", and got permission from the author to use it in the hotel's promotional materials. Regretfully, Maugham at first had to decline Schutzman's impulsive invitation to stay at the Raffles as his guest, since he was getting too old and "I don't think I will ever travel that far again."

But five years later he reconsidered and in 1959 announced to Schutzman in a letter that he would be pleased to take him at his word, as he would be coming out on a farewell tour of the Far East. When the hotel management refused to honour the obligation, Schutzman paid for the room out of his own pocket.

The inimitable, albeit not always lovable, Schutzman has never been duplicated at the Raffles since his departure. His assistant Mario Marchesi became Raffles' third Italian manager. Much of Schutzman's style had rubbed off on him, but he exhibited less of his former boss's *hauteur*, lacked his almost aristocratic outlook.

Born in 1914 in Rome, Mario was a professional hotelier and in 1963 was one of 42 nominees for the title "favourite hotel manager" nominated by the American Society of Travel Agents of Southern California. A more perplexing award was that of the title of "Admiral" of the non-existent navy of Nebraska, jocularly bestowed upon him by the Governor of Nebraska, Mr E. Robinson, in 1965. Only one other hotelier had been thus honoured before, the manager of

Tokyo's Imperial Hotel.

Mario it was who in 1965 first saw the wisdom of issuing Raffles Hotel spoons and key chains—about 1,000 a year—to souvenir hunters, so as to stem the tourism theft that is bound to go on in any hotel as famous as Raffles.

In the 1950s', the powerful local Oversea Chinese Banking Corporation, with prominent banker and politician Tan Chin Tuan at its helm as managing director since 1942, had bought control of the hotel company.

The 1960s saw both newly independent Singapore and the Raffles Hotel floundering around for a new identity, a new role in a rapidly changing world, and unfortunately none of the managers of this period seems to have got a real grip on the problem.

It was a knotty problem: how was a grand old lady like Raffles to compete with the flashy glass and concrete jobs springing up all over Singapore "like bamboo shoots in the spring rain" to use a Chinese saying, with the brash young Singaporean cock-a-hoop at his economic success, his "modernity" and his freedom from his former colonial masters, and consequently remarkably uncaring about his own history? In any event, the way he saw it, the Raffles's history was not his at all, but that of his British overlords. It would have taken an extraordinary manager indeed to overcome such psychological barriers.

The present manager, Roberto Pregarz, Raffles' fourth Italian manager since 1972, has not, however, been content to allow its affairs to become static; he has restored something of the Sarkies' original personal style to his charge.

One rarely finds one's way to Roberto blocked by a secretary, certainly not by a public relations officer, for he is truly accessible in his humble little brown office off the lobby. He is utterly absorbed in the hotel's history and has spent many hours in reference libraries reconstructing as much as he can.

One of his most recent projects has been the creation of a small Raffles Museum in the hotel, where all the "Rafflesiana", all the memorabilia he has been able to muster are stored. Among its contents are chinaware still bearing the Sarkies Brothers' company logo consisting of the entwined initials "SB", odd pieces of cutlery stamped with the Rangoon Strand monogram, old books, all the newspaper articles ever written about the hotel (which amount to a veritable mountain of paper), photos and many other souvenirs to serve as backdrop for the audio-visual show which he himself has compiled to explain the hotel's history.

What was once the Raffles' weak point—its age—Roberto has made its strongest selling point, even if it does mean keeping on some seemingly antediluvian waiters. It is he who, without proper regard to effective land-use ratios or air-conditioning bills—thank goodness—has restored the hotel's original high ceilings and resuscitated the old ceiling fans, uncovered old tiles in the Tiffin Room, installed delightfully dated music in the Palm Court.

Maintenance is of course a problem—but not such a tough one when you have

Roberto and Helena Pregarz, the present manager and his wife, in the Palm Court.
By courtesy of Times Periodicals Ptd Ltd.

a manager who is willing to rush off, screwdriver and pliers in hand, to fix broken light switches for himself, as he often does.

There is still something of the zany one-man band touch about him, indeed. Asked to find a particular old menu or photo, he will dive into the pile of tattered paper threatening to overwhelm his desk, files tumbled wildly one on top of the other, ferret furiously around and finally emerge triumphant, waving the required item. "I never throw anything away", he says proudly. Which is just as well, for one gets the uneasy feeling that he may not always know what he has at the bottom of that tantalising pile of "rubbish".

He is far from cool and calm, but then, he would be untrue to his Latin blood if he were.

Trieste-born Roberto Pregarz is at Raffles primarily because in 1967 he, a seasoned sailor, got seasick. In charge of the floating restaurants on the Lloyd Triestino line for 10 years, he met Mario Marchesi in Hongkong and was offered the job of assistant manager in 1967. He didn't take the bait until six months later when rough waters in the Mediterranean made him so seasick "I wanted to die." He was understandably at his most vulnerable shortly after this, when a letter, with job contract and air ticket to Singapore, arrived from Mario Marchesi. "That did it. Anything would be better than another cruise like the last one, so I came to Singapore. And never looked back."

Today he is very much part of the Singapore scene, not least because, helped just a little by the general tourism boom, he has increased the Raffles occupancy rate from 34 percent to 91 percent since 1972.

He is deeply attached both to the Raffles and to Singapore, which has given him his Chinese wife. Helena, and his little son Andrea—or An-de, which means "peaceful virtue". Helena, endowed with an artistic bent, has covered the walls of the Raffles with her sketches, decoupages and wool-embroidered tapestries on themes from the hotel's history.

Now Roberto's strong Italian accent is overlaid with a hint of "Singapore English", and he admits "I have found a family and it makes me very happy. Chinese New Year is a big event for me now—I pay my respects to my Chinese elders."

Understandably, he does not like to be thought of as a foreigner nowadays. But he has received several foreign decorations, including the rank of *Cavaliere* from the Italian government for contributions to the hotel industry, awarded in 1975, which effectively means he has been knighted, and the *Timone d'Oro* (Golden Helm) from the international tourism body Borsa Internationale Turismo in Italy, for his assistance to an Italian film crew making *The Tigers of Malaya*.

But while Roberto has been helping to train a new generation of hoteliers and waiters at the Hotel and Catering Training School which he partly founded, the older generation still pads its discreet and sometimes ponderous way among the diners at the Raffles. To meet them, we must leave the manager's office and go backstage.

7 BEHIND THE SCENES: THE STAFF

The greatest virtue of an Asian servant—or "Asiatic" as he used to be known in the Singapore of old—was, as far as his master was concerned, an ability to be as invisible as possible.

The generally offhand attitude to downstairs "non-persons" has been noted in a previous chapter. It was so universally accepted among whites that the author of a 1927 handbook to British Malaya could unblushingly assure his readers that there was "no real lack of fairly efficient household labour if the employer is not unreasonably exacting" and add: "The Oriental is, however, not accustomed, and never will be accustomed, to the hard work about the house which many housewives themselves perform in Europe, and is by nature not given to worrying much over small matters, so that an equable temperament is very desirable in an employer if the domestic machine is to run smoothly."

The first waiters at the Raffles were probably clad in uniform originating from India—turban, tunic and puttees—as were most servants in the elegant European households of late nineteenth-century Singapore. Their garb had acquired a more local flavour, although still very colourful, by 1964 at least, when Noel Coward referred to the Raffles roomboys in his short story *Pretty Polly Barlow* as resplendent in blue sarongs and red jackets. (His story was to form the kernel of the film "Pretty Polly" shot at the Raffles in 1967, starring Hayley Mills and Trevor Howard.)

Snapping of the fingers, or loudly called, imperious summonses by people unfamiliar with the mores of the Orient were, unknown to them, treated with cold contempt by waiters and room attendants. Polite recognition of the dignity of servants was rewarded with courteous, smooth and efficient service that not even the most munificent tip could extract from a "boy" who considered himself superior to the vulgar guest.

It is precisely this delicately balanced relationship of mutual respect between master and servant, each party "knowing his place", that continues to baffle the outsider and still obtains in historical establishments such as the Raffles. The more democratic, even radical, tone of recent decades, especially in the West, has caused many to condemn such customs as nothing more or less than rank "feudalism", a shameful thing which should be abolished, or at least hidden from view.

But only those who participate in such relationships can know the very real affection engendered between the *tuan* (master) and his servant, when each gets the respect he thinks he deserves. To understand the staff at the Raffles, you need to understand this old colonial formula; to the newcomer, the old waiters in the Elizabethan Grill or the Palm Court, almost to a man plying the traditional trade of their Hainanese Chinese forefathers, may appear surly, slow, even incom-

Staff photo 1940s.
Front, extreme left: Quek Chua Khoon, cashier; second left: Tan Geck Swee, now chief cashier; Ang Ann Lian, chief clerk; assistant manager Ernest Smith; chief accountant Miss Barnett; Nino Cevenini; manager Guido Cevenini (moustashioed); German supervisor, Klauk; storekeeper William J. Collick; receptionist KR Samy. By courtesy of Tan Geok Swee and the Raffles Hotel; taken by the Raffles photographers

petent. A visiting British journalist wrote of them quite recently that they "went about their business with the unsmiling deliberation of patrolling sentries". Yet at the sight of an old regular, whom they never fail to recognise no matter how long ago their last meeting, they will be transformed, attentive, agile even, and wreathed in smiles; even more so if a word of colonially-accented Malay or Chinese is tossed their way.

Many of the staff are too old to change. But they are an inseparable component of the Raffles mystique. None the less, as the social structure in Singapore changed during the 1930s, it is true that some whites clung over-insistently to their privileges, or else they were gross parvenus, unschooled in the subtleties of the master-servant relationship. They began to abuse this relationship, blithely ignoring shifting realities in Singapore and in the world beyond.

The Raffles staff became distinctly apathetic, service at the hotel hitting an all-time low just before the Japanese occupation. But by the end of the war the British were seen as saviours, through the rosy spectacles of the 1945 liberation.

Even now many older Singaporeans, Raffles staff in particular, will tell you confidentially, their voices lowered as though it is "not quite nice" as a true-blue Singaporean to say so, that the "good old days" under the British were better, gayer, had more "style".

"Ah, Christmas then was really Christmas", sighs former chief cashier Tan Geok Swee, "We really felt it then—crackers, 'Midnight Surprise' and all . . . !"

The staff feel that in independent Singapore, their own status has been undermined, with the days of the long gown balls gone. They are, secretly, personally affronted at the sight of jeans and sandals in "their" hotel.

Long service has been a characteristic of the Raffles staff—in 1952, 18 employees retired with an average of 21 years' service each, one totalling as many as 49 years, and others 30 or more.

Not that the staff has always been utterly compliant. They started to "get smart" as their education improved in the 1930s and 1940s. Guests with a smattering of Malay who used phrases in the indigenous language to order from a waiter, hall porter, or room servant would pointedly receive a reply in impeccable English. And if the order was given in English, the response would be in Malay, just to emphasise that the recipient was as bilingual, or more so, than the person addressing him.

A condescending attitude was no longer tolerated, and any remaining subservience came to an abrupt full stop in the 1950s and early 1960s, when, like most labour in Singapore, the Raffles staff became completely disaffected, organising several strikes, which must have made life at the Raffles very difficult for both managers and guests.

In the 1950s the Raffles was struggling to make up for lost time, spending heavily on modernisation, so the strikes could hardly have come at a worse time for the operating company, and they struck the hotel's overall viability a heavy blow. Ironically, in 1951 the company had started a staff provident fund for the first time, with a basic company donation of almost $18,000, into which staff could if they wished pay five percent of their salaries as a savings-pension measure.

But the 330 staff went on a five-day strike in 1955, leaving volunteers, airline hostesses and the guests to "do it themselves" in running the Raffles.

In 1960 the hotel management paid the staff an 80 percent bonus, amounting to more than $30,000, after one week's negotiations with the SGEU (Singapore General Employees' Union).

But matters got worse in the 1960s, for the Secretary of the union was a radical, Dominic Puthucheary, brother of an even more prominent revolutionary, James Puthucheary. Both are now in virtual exile in Kuala Lumpur, after serving terms of detention without trial in prison. The Puthucheary brothers and their friends were bent on tipping to the left the fine balance struck by the uneasy left-moderate coalition then ruling Singapore as the united People's Action Party, under Prime Minister Lee Kuan Yew.

Staff photo, February 3, 1950.
Former chief cashier Swee is front row, number 8 from left; storekeeper W. J. Collick number 10, Guido Cevenini, manager, in centre (14 from left, moustachioed) with his brother Nino next to him; and the popular Reception staff KR Samy at number 17 from left, standing directly behind Miss Barnett (chief accountant, on the left of Guido Cevenini, in front row); in second row is cashier Quek Chua Khoon.
By courtesy of Quek Chua Khoon and the Raffles Hotel.

Raffles's employees indulged in a work-to-rule tactic, taking three-hour lunch breaks on several occasions during 1960 and 1961, ostensibly to discuss the bonus issue. The hotel management was forced to serve free sandwiches and soft drinks for lunch.

As the hotel's culinary reputation consequently plummeted, it was hardly surprising that in late 1961 the management seemed to yield: the staff, now numbering about 400, got increments of between $10 and $40 a head, back-dated three months, but with the management winning the proviso that the hotel's future income and profits justify any further such awards. This agreement also gave the staff medical insurance benefits for the first time.

In his 1961 annual report, chairman Tan Chin Tuan rumbled ominously: "The hotel is fortunate in having assembled a large number of employees who are not only fully trained but also long in service and extremely loyal. It is the policy of the company to treat its staff as well, if not better, than those in comparable businesses, but unfortunately, during the year, unnecessarily protracted negotiations with the staff union have tended to leave the company in doubt as to the wisdom of embarking on modernising the hotel on a big scale, let alone rebuilding it . . ."

There was talk at that time of building a new Raffles on a site next to the Singapore Swimming Club. But Mr Tan spoke in vain: in 1963, a strike by the entire, communist-controlled Singapore Association of Trade Unions hit both hotels and cinemas, taking workers out not only at the Raffles, but also at a number of other hotels.

Pluckily optimistic, manager Mario Marchesi nonetheless continued to accept bookings.

The staff of the Raffles must have been considered a desirable prize by the unions, for a contest between the Singapore Restaurants, Bars, Eating and Coffee Shop Employees' Union and the Singapore Manual and Mercantile Workers' Union arose in 1964, which resulted in the former winning the right, by 114 votes to 106, to represent the Raffles workers. The SGEU had by then been officially de-registered for its agitation, along with two other unions.

The situation began to settle down in 1963 after the People's Action Party put more than 100 leftist agitators inside for an indefinite term, without trial, under a police swoop ominously tagged "Operation Cold Store" and then went on to win a decisive election victory over the left in the same year.

A commission of inquiry into the de-registered unions' financial affairs in 1964 reported that some SGEU officials had been guilty of virtual extortion from members, including the Raffles staff, exacting from them far more than the usual union subscription fee. After their 1960 bonus agreement with the Raffles management, the staff had for example been asked to "donate" $5 a head to the union. Albert de Silva, the Portuguese-Eurasian assistant secretary of the SGEU's Raffles Hotel branch in 1959, told the commission that although the hotel employees had been "victimised" in the past, the union had turned out to be as bad.

Only four months before Singapore's "separation" from Malaysia in August 1965 (it was really an expulsion) the Raffles staff and their union signed a full collective agreement with the management, in which a wage scale was fixed.

In 1968 any residual labour unrest was quieted for a long while to come by the passing of Singapore's tough new labour laws.

The staff remaining today do not say much about these turbulent days. While the crude stereotype of the "inscrutable Oriental" is an inaccurate representation of the Chinese in general, but even more so of the expressive Singapore Chinese, it is true that the type of man who works at the Raffles has been trained not to notice even the most embarrassing facts, and to "pretend it didn't happen".

Others among the staff cannot tell one much about what happened at the hotel, not so much because they have conveniently forgotten as because they really could not have seen much of what went on outside their own narrow little preserve, whether that was the kitchen or the reception desk.

As far as Bok Siang Han, for example, is concerned, life pretty much boils down to filleting fish, which is what he does best. A Hainanese born of a peasant family in China—one of the staff reckons that roughly 90 percent of the Raffles staff is Hainanese, the Chinese dialect group traditionally dominating the restaurant trade—Siang Han was still, at the time of writing, working in the Raffles kitchen, the longest-serving member of staff.

He started as a teenager in the long gone Hotel de l'Europe in the 1930s, having arrived in Singapore in a Chinese junk, an illiterate without any schooling, his pockets distinctly unlined. He knows his father once travelled to and from Southeast Asia a lot, but does not know what he did; only that he died on board ship just as his son, Siang Han, was born.

When the Europe closed down in the early 1930s, he moved to the Raffles, specialising in fish dishes, for about $30 a month, with no limits fixed to his working hours. Unmarried staff in those days lived in a one-room dormitory at the hotel: it still exists, and is used today as a staff restroom.

A jolly character, the perfect image of what a cook should be, Siang Han's real work is only the preparation of foodstuffs, not the actual cooking. In Chinese cooking, however, much of the art, and the work, lies in the preparation. European food is much easier for him but, as he now remarks, reflecting the social changes in the post-colonial era: "Today, people eat more Chinese food."

"Keeping it in the family" is a very Chinese characteristic which the Raffles tends to perpetuate. There could be no better illustration of this than the fact that Ngiams have tended the Long Bar since the first of the line, Ngiam Tong Boon, invented that heady concoction the Singapore Sling in 1915.

The present incumbent, Robert Ngiam, has been high priest for 25 years of the esoteric order that mixes this and other famous cocktails at Raffles.

The most articulate old hand among the recent staff is Tan Geok Swee, an English-educated "Straits Chinese" who retired as chief cashier in 1980, having worked in the hotel since 1936. His grandfather came to Singapore from Amoy in China's southern Fukien province. His father was a partner in a grocery shop in the Tanjong Pagar area, Singapore's old dockland. Later he went into a small coffee powder business, importing beans from Bali, but this enterprise collapsed, leaving 18-year-old Geok Swee destitute when his father died at the age of 66.

"I had to struggle to feed my 55-year-old mother", he recalls, the unselfish emphasis typical of traditional Chinese filial respect.

Staff photo, 1950s.
Front row, extreme left: one of the Manasseh girls, popular local entertainers. Left to right, Mrs Bertha Mathieson (wife of a Danish assistant manager), Sylvia and Mario Marchesi (manager-to-be), accountant Ang Ann Lian, manager Frans Schutzman, Miss Theodora Henderson, storekeeper W. J. Collick, S. O. Seng, chief cashier Tan Geok Swee and Stephen Wee, later secretary to Marchesi.
By courtesy of Quek Chua Khoon and the Raffles Hotel

After stints as a supervisor on a small rubber estate and as a fitter with a car firm, he joined the Raffles at $60 a month in 1936 as a general clerk, a job which he says left him no time or money to think of getting married until the ripe old age, by Chinese standards, of 31. (This was a marriage arranged in haste to a distant relative when his mother, who lay dying of cancer, said she felt it was a "shame" on the family that her son should still be unmarried.)

In his new job at the Raffles, he says quite frankly, "I was bullied at first. There was no union then—we worked long hours and were exploited. I would work till late at night—I didn't know what is enjoyment. And the British were very *Tuan Besar* (Big Boss, in Malay) and very snobbish in those days." Today, Geok Swee still blinks benignly through his specs in his Singapore home, but rather wonders if he wouldn't prefer to have the old days—and the British—back after all. He delights in showing you his impressive collection of autographs from some of Raffles' more famous guests.

Another cashier, Quek Chua Koon, who joined the hotel in 1946, has similarly taken advantage of his position to gather autographs.

The staff of any hotel represent a microcosm of humanity, so some employees have been up to dishonest tricks from time to time, but not as frequently as might be expected in view of the maximum opportunity hotel workers have. One former staff member was taken to court for cheating Sarkies Martyrose Arathoon of $83 in the form of hotel cash chits: while in 1957 the chief receptionist at the time pleaded guilty and was placed on probation for two years for taking $9,623 from the hotel by issuing cash chits in a hotel director's name.

Staff feuds are pursued at a subterranean level until they force themselves to the surface. One such feud may have been the background to what happened when an Indian driver attached to the hotel died in 1947 after his bed had mysteriously caught fire early one Sunday morning. The police detained another Indian employee for interrogation, even though he had dutifully run from the bedroom shouting, "*Api, api*'" (Fire, fire!)

The diminutive "buttons" mentioned earlier, who used to slip cards into the palms of improperly dressed gentlemen on the Raffles dance floor, requesting them to leave, was another well remembered hotel personality.

Former colonial government officer Andrew Gilmour also recalls a small flower seller posted at the hotel entrance in pre-war days, and spotted him again in later years, a "wizened old 'daftie' who prowls about the Padang in a white uniform bowed down with phoney medals." One can only speculate on what may have happened in the interim, to reduce him to this.

Maybe he, or another "buttons", was the smart little fellow who in the 1920s was an early exponent of the art of what is today known as "moonlighting"— holding down two jobs. An orphan, he used the money he earned by attending to the needs of the hotel's guests to pay the fees for his education at the old Raffles Institution, a school which formerly adjoined the hotel.

The tradition of hotel "character" is perpetuated now by the doormen in their topees, flanked by flower-sellers and a persuasive itinerant chiropodist, by the affable and elegant supervisor, Mr Ang Seng Chor, by charming young girl receptionists, and by that army of discreet chambermaids and roomboys that goes to make up the backbone of Raffles—its 270 staff.

8 THE "CLUB"

To have stayed at the Raffles is to have joined illustrious company, an exclusive "club", although it must be granted that there has been the occasional black sheep among the members, an élite comprising kings, princes, politicians and movie stars.

At the start, the Sarkies seem to have relied very much on snob appeal to promote their hotel. Press advertisements during the 1890s and at the turn of the century consisted almost entirely of interminable lists of weighty names—most of which, however, are virtually unknown to the present day reader.

The public was breathlessly informed that the guest list had included the names of the Duke of Newcastle, the Earl of Dysart, Lord and Lady Braye, Lord Dormer, Lord Cecil, and Lord Valletort, among others.

Repressing the urge to murmur "Who?", one reads on to find an even more impressive list of foreign royalty—the Grand Duke Cyril of Russia, Prince Adalbert of Germany, Princes Kan-in and Iwakura of Japan, Princes Damrong and Tugala of Siam, and the Maharajas of Gwalior and Kapurthala. In Victorian times, the overweening respect for royalty of almost any colour, so long as its blood was true-blue, seems to have overridden any latent tendency towards that racial discrimination that marked later decades.

Naturally local dignitaries were also listed as patrons—Sir Frank Swettenham, Resident-General of the Federated Malay States, and Sir John Anderson, Governor of the Straits Settlements, among them.

A great number of military gentlemen seem to have patronised the Raffles at this time—Major-General Sir Henry Collett, KCB; Brigadier-General Gossit, CB; Major-General Sir Charles Warren, GCMG, KCB, RE; Major-General Molyneux; Major-General Jones Vaughan "Commanding the Troops, SS'; General Sir A R F Dorward, KCB, DSO; Admirals Sir Henry Keppel (after whom Singapore's Keppel Road and Keppel Harbour are still named); Sir Cyprian Bridge and Sir Henry Seymour, to name but a few.

It was the report of one such military guest's sojourn at the Raffles which first led to the hotel's being tagged "The Savoy of Singapore". London's *The Sphere* magazine coined this catch-phrase in March 1905, reporting on "Russia's Rout: men who have failed to check it".

General Stoessel, a Russian general prominent in the 1905 Russo-Japanese campaigns, was pictured in the article "as he tiffined with the Russian consul at Raffles Hotel, the Savoy of Singapore". The caption also dubbed Stoessel "defender of Port Arthur", which strategic point near Vladivostock the Russians had earlier grabbed from its rightful owner, China, and which fell to the Japanese in 1905. It must have been a somewhat lugubrious lunch for, as *The Sphere* remarked meaningfully, "Stoessel has had his audience with the Czar"—i.e.,

The Sphere, March 18, 1905, showing Russian General Stoessel at the Raffles. By courtesy of the British Library

been carpeted for Russia's rout. Sure enough, the faces on the photo are unsmiling.

But "Meet me at the Raffles" thereafter became as fashionable an injunction as "Meet me at the Savoy".

Singapore was a small town and the press found the most trivial event worthy of its attention—it would have been difficult to stay at the Raffles and still evade such attention.

Not only did Lord Henry Frederick Thynne, second son of the Marquis of Bath and treasurer of the British Queen's household 1875–1880, as well as Member of Parliament for South Wiltshire from 1859 to 1885, and "now on a trip around the world", merit mention in the *Straits Times* of March 18, 1898 as one of Raffles' guests, but so did, a year earlier, the Misses Edie and Nellie Bibby, "the charming daughters of the veteran manager of the Raub Mines, Malaya", who were heralded as "heroines of a record-breaking adventure". Their adventure, which would not greatly impress young travellers today, consisted of "meandering along the eastern coast of the Malay Peninsula". "And", gasped the *Straits Times*, "they are the very first Anglo-Saxon daughters of Eve who have been seen by their duskier sisters in Kelantan" (a Malayan state).

Another notable guest, in January 1899, was a Siamese nobleman, His Excellency Phya Sukhum, accompanied by his private secretary, Luang Pinit, en route for Calcutta. He was described as being "deeply versed in the writings upon and history of Buddha", and he had been deputed by the King of Siam to proceed to India to investigate relics of Buddha discovered there the previous year, and to receive such of them as the Government of India had made gifts of to his Siamese Majesty. We can be pardoned the assumption that he may well have returned home via the Raffles and that the hotel may therefore once have played host to Buddha himself—or rather, to parts of him.

Naturally, not all guests were intent on such holy business. From time to time, the Raffles would be inundated by the somewhat rowdy overspill from fun-fairs or circuses on the reclamation ground opposite, just as it was later to dread, in its haughty fashion, the regular "invasions" from the 1950s onwards by the other-rank soldiers frequenting the British Naafi opposite the hotel.

In celebration of the approaching coronation of King Edward VII in 1902, a fair started up on "ye greate space of grounds in front of Raffles Hys Inne, weather permittynge", as a whimsical poster announced. The hotel was invaded at dusk by what one participant called "the most awful collection of apparitions that possibly it had ever seen, for of course everyone was wet through with exertion". The "apparitions" included nigger minstrels, a fat lady and a quack doctor.

The managers of that early Raffles were just as harrassed by embarrassing incidents and the resulting bad press as any manager today, indeed more so.

Particularly mortifying to the management must have been the "strange fatality" of 12 June, 1895, when Mr McBreen, an usher in the local magistrate's court, "dropped down dead" at 11.15 pm while playing billiards at the Raffles. This event was apparently of sufficient moment as to justify an inquiry by the Governor, no less.

Similarly, in 1896 the manager, one M. Joaqim, had to deal with a call saying that "a gentleman was in the passage very sick". Mr David Traille Robertson, the new accountant at the Chartered Bank, had poisoned himself accidentally, the coroner ruled.

That some hotel guests turned out to be rogues who skipped the joint without paying their dues has already been discussed. The press of the 1890s was also full of reports of minor thefts from hotel guests—just one more indication of what a 'Wild West town' early Singapore must have been.

The Vice-consul for the Netherlands and a Mr Anderson of Mansfield and Co were among the many in the 1890s who were robbed of gold trinkets such as watches or chains, left in their rooms at the Raffles. Security was slack in those days and dishonest "boys" were the bane of the age, if we are to believe the press. One Malayan planter's "boy" absconded from the Raffles with his master's property in a ship called *Malacca*.

Many Europeans made a habit of travelling with their own servants in those days, it seems, which must have relieved the Raffles staff of some of their more onerous duties.

One robbery provoked a protracted and rancorous correspondence in the *Straits Times* during February-March 1898, between Mr J. S. Ransome, special correspondent for the London *Morning Post*, staying at the Raffles (still a top favourite with journalists today), and Joaqim, the hotel manager.

The newspaper reported that his watch (missing with papers, money and jewellery) was taken from under his pillow while he slept—a point that was rejected by the manager, who said this was not true: the timepiece was taken from the table.

This was only adding fuel to the fire, for Ransome then wrote in sarcastic vein that he was quite willing to accept the view suggested by his letter that some of the employees knew a great deal more about the robbery than the police, himself, or anyone else. He added that the hotel very promptly and apparently without difficulty found and returned the empty box and nearly all the valueless portion of the stolen articles.

Reluctantly, we must discount some of the claims relating to famous guests at the Raffles in the early days. As we have already seen, the hotel did not really achieve even its physical zenith until its renovation in 1899, and even then was constantly overshadowed by the smarter Europe until its rival was closed in the 1930s. Rudyard Kipling, as already remarked, probably did not stay more than a night at the Raffles, just enough to convince him that the experience was not worth repeating, even though the food was good.

One man who almost certainly did not stay at the Raffles was Joseph Conrad. It has been said that he was inspired to write *Lord Jim* while reading a newspaper report at the Raffles, but while there is room for some debate over whether he perhaps may once have had a tipple at the hotel, the evidence for anything more does not stand up to examination. The relevant dates make it quite impossible that *Lord Jim*, written about 1900, could have been "born" in the Raffles.

The incident which inspired Conrad's tale of the pilgrim ship *Patna*, abandoned on the high seas by its officers and crew, with passengers still aboard, and the resulting public inquiry at "an Eastern port" (Singapore, contend some authorities), took place in August 1880. The real ship's name was *Jeddah*, and it belonged to the Singapore Steamship Co., managed by Syed Muhammad Alsagoff, a member of the wealthy Arab family which was later to control large stretches of Beach Road, including parts of the Raffles Hotel site.

But, as we already know, the hotel was not even taken over by the Sarkies until 1887, and Conrad anyway paid only three fairly brief visits to Singapore, between 1883 and 1887. It is more likely that he read of the *Patna* case while in London in 1880 and was again reminded of it first in 1883 when the *Jeddah* once again sailed into Singapore harbour, and yet again when the Alsagoffs put the ship up for sale in Singapore, disguised as the *Diamond*. Both events occasioned considerable press comment at the time.

Conrad probably stayed at the Sailor's Home and occasionally frequented "dives" such as the Tingle Tangle, with its attractive East European hostesses offering the female company a sailor would surely have needed on his rare shore visits.

The Malabar Hotel described in *Lord Jim* almost certainly was the Europe. A reading of Norman Sherry's *Conrad's Eastern World* is sufficient reasonably to convince one of this interpretation.

But came the 1920s and 1930s, and the hotel was full of exotic characters.

Local journalist Harry "Hoppy" Hopkin who stayed there through the 1920s indulged, according to his own account, in a little romance—"strictly platonic, of course!"—with an opera singer, a woman novelist, a girl who was a magician's assistant and was nightly sawn in half, a musical comedy lead and various tourists. He said the Russian guests were of a fascinating variety, some claiming mysteriously to have titles, to be refugees from the old regime.

But the Raffles was above all the venue for the planters down for a rest and binge from their lonely estates in the jungles of Malaya. "They came to kick over the traces a bit", says former assistant manager, Ernest Smith. So important was their custom to the hotel that they got a special discount on the usual room rate of $8 a day for a single room or $15 for a double. However, not all of them were as badly behaved as rumour has alleged—Tan Geok Swee even says, "They were well behaved", although he admits they "liked their drink"; journalist Ian Morrison said in the 1940s that he came across a few cases of the "whisky-swilling planter" but on the whole this was a fiction invented by those who had never been to Malaya.

However, those with an appetite for the spice of scandal need not feel too frustrated, for there were plenty of incidents of the nature they enjoy.

Malaysian royalty has been counted among the many blue-blooded guests at the Raffles.

Among the most frequent, and most respected, royal visitors at the Raffles were the Anglophile Sultans of Johor, descendants of the original prince who first struck the deal handing Singapore island over to Sir Stamford Raffles in 1819. Fabulously wealthy, they were avid party-goers, coming over to the Raffles from their resplendent palaces across the Causeway in Malaya, as it then was. They had, and still have, substantial property and land-holdings in Singapore, where they built in particular their European-style residence at Tyersall, in fashionable Tanglin.

At the Raffles guests and staff alike would look forward to the social sparkle—not to mention the monetary sort—which the Sultan and his retinue would bring with them. One staunch buddy of his was Frank Buck, of "Bring 'Em Back Alive" fame, a fellow Raffles regular.

Doris Geddes of The Little Boutique at the Raffles, who was very much in with the Sultan's "in-crowd", designed the coronation gown for his new Sultanah, Lady Marcella, a statuesque woman of East European extraction, in 1955. She was crowned with platinum and diamonds, in what was described as a ceremony of pomp, splendour and rich pageantry at which she wore a magnificent coronation gown of pink and silver . . . a combination of East and West.

"Glittering" was certainly a reasonable adjective—both literally and metaphorically—to apply to the company any Raffles guest might find himself keeping in those days. Besides the royals of Johor, there were the Brookes—the "white rajahs" of Sarawak in Borneo ever since their grandfather James Brooke, a former British East India Company official turned adventurer, had put down a rebellion in the area in 1838 and been appointed ruler by the Sultan of Brunei, suzerain of Sarawak.

The Ranee of Sarawak and her three lovely daughters frequently hove into Singapore, and the Raffles, in pre-war days. Judging from some accounts, they had themselves a whale of a time. They adored dancing and dazzled the young men who clustered around them. The Brookes were to lose their hereditary grip on Sarawak in 1946, when the country was annexed for the British Crown. Today, it is part of Malaysia.

Local luminaries also abounded at the Raffles, in full finery. Although almost no Asians actually stayed there during these class-conscious decades, the wealthy *Babas*, Straits Chinese, who effectively acted as local intermediaries for the British in the colonial government, were high-profile on the Raffles ballroom floor at important functions.

Particularly well remembered among the *Babas* is Mrs "Pansy" Lee Choon Guan, wife of a member of the Legislative Council, which being official and nominated, was little more than a testing ground for, and organ of, colonial government policy, but which nonetheless carried considerable social clout in those days.

Pansy, it seems, was chiefly noted for her diamonds, of which she would wear a solid collar on occasions such as the Christmas Eve or New Year's Eve dances. Doris Geddes also remembered Pansy's jacket with five 12-carat diamond buttons, worn one evening at a private film show, possibly held in the hotel for the Sultan of Johor and his retinue. "She looked like a torchlight in the darkness", said Doris.

Lesser lights passing through the hotel would cause an equal stir in their own ways. There were the rugger rowdies homing in on the bar after a match, the "sacrilegious, outrageous bunch of drunken hoodlums" which overspilled into the ballroom after a Singapore University Ball in the late 1950s, and the New Zealander who, inspired by the grape, vaulted over rows of dining tables along the full length of the dining room, without distrubing so much as a teaspoon. Not to mention the angry Italian *donna* who in full public view stuffed a 30-carat ruby down the throat of her lover, Count Pojaloff.

Then there was the fellow who, given the sack and a "one-way ticket home" for questionable business transactions on his own account outside of his employers' firm, had the brass to leave his erstwhile bosses holding the bill for his farewell whoopee at the Raffles. "Not only did the bill include several dozen oysters, bottles of champagne and expensive liqueurs but also the cost of repair and replacement of several articles of furniture", said a friend of his.

Another ingenious guest faked a dramatic fall down the sweeping staircase near the ballroom in order so to frighten the litigation-shy manager, Mario Marchesi, that his room bill was waived, yet had the cheek to turn up at the Adelphi Hotel soon after looking as right as rain. The Raffles's doctor, Charles Wilson, made sure to get him blackballed at the Adelphi too, having done some inspired detective work on the heel marks left by the culprit on the staircase.

Why did they all stay at the Raffles? Perhaps Dr Wilson has the answer: "While having a meal with a very wealthy American, I asked him why he always stayed there. He said it was indefinable; it was the old worldliness of it, the warm feeling, the graciousness. Just then his roomboy came and said, 'Tuan, would you change your *dhoby* (laundry) list? There was a black sock in the toe of a shoe, there were three more handkerchiefs I found in a suit . . . another pair of underclothes in the bathroom!'

"The chit was duly amended. And the roomboy then said, 'Your cufflinks are now correct and I have ordered a new set of laces for your brown shoes.' I sat there very impressed, but I hope I did not show it. And my American friend said, 'Now you know why I stay at Raffles. There is no hotel in the world where you get treatment like that.'"

Some of the guests were just peculiar. Take the man whom some remember to be called Baron Empin, for example. He was, apparently, a Belgian with business interests in the Middle East, who would arrive in the 1930s on his private yacht "with a lot of young people aboard", as Ernest Smith tells it. "He was a bit peculiar—he would get them all to dress in sailors' costumes. He dressed as the captain and would bring about 30 of them to the hotel for lunch."

Apparently, the Baron's personal preoccupation was to find, among his many girl friends, a suitable mother for his son and heir. When he heard by cable that he had at last been made a father, he immediately left the hotel and flew to Paris, leaving his guests and the yacht behind in order to remove his child from its mother since he "did not approve of her".

Another regular but out-of-the-ordinary visitor in the 1920s and 1930s was Dr Serge Voronoff, the Russian discoverer of the monkey gland process of rejuvenation so talked about at that time. Ernest Smith clearly remembers him, already at least middle-aged, checking into the hotel register as "Dr and Mrs Voronoff" with one of the most beautiful statuesque blondes he had ever seen, and whom he had taken for his daughter. "I thought that was quite a recommendation for monkey glands, myself!" he says.

But one man's quite literally huge presence loomed larger than life over other guests during the crazy 1920s and 1930s—that of the noted archaeologist and historian, Professor Pieter van Stein Callenfels, a towering six-foot-four-inches—tall, 24-stone giant of a man "on a Brobdingnagian scale", as Malayan civil servant Victor Purcell portrayed him.

Callenfels was the Dutchman who has since been enshrined in the Raffles mythology for allegedly consuming 10 bottles of gin at breakfast. This is most likely a slight, but solidly-based, exaggeration. Certainly the fact remains that Callenfels possessed a staggering appetite for beer. He drank it by the dozen bottles at a sitting and it was an insult to offer him less than a quart at a time, according to Purcell. His record for beer consumed at one sitting was said to be 35 bottles. A hotelier's dream, or nightmare?

He had an appetite for food to match, but, in order not to overwhelm the reader with his monstrous personality, I shall leave the awesome details to my discussion of gastronomic matters in the next chapter.

Perhaps more interesting were the inevitable anatomical consequences of his gourmandise. Newsman R. C. H. McKie, who observed him at the Raffles, said that he "overflowed the chair in vast undulations of flesh which started from his pregnant paunch and rolled downwards, upwards and sideways." He carried on conversation in a stentorian voice that could be heard a hundred yards away and which "blew his beard aside and his monstrous body heaved and shuddered like a shaken blancmange".

Callenfels however did precious little to mitigate his unappealing physique. He wore curry-stained pyjamas at all times of the day and his calloused feet bore testimony to the fact that he wore shoes only on ceremonial occasions. He used to boast that he had his hair cut once a year—always on his birthday.

His beard, nicotined from chain-smoking Filipino hand-made cigarillos while explaining himself to his audiences in four languages, was tangled and unkempt. His favourite audience was made up of women, whom he addressed like half-wits, said Purcell.

Callenfels lectured often on his subject, which he practised largely in Indonesia, where, a Leiden University graduate, he had begun around 1900 as a cadet in the Dutch colonial civil service, later serving as director of the Netherlands East Indies Government's archaeological department.

He turned coffee-planter for a while but simultaneously pursued his anthropological and archaeological vocation, leading to his second government appointment. He was darkly rumoured to have once lived with the cannibals of Sumatra and to have eaten human flesh—he does sound as though he might have eaten almost anything!

The original model for Sir Arthur Conan Doyle's Professor Challenger, hero of *The Lost World*, Callenfels was also loved for the eyes which twinkled behind thick glasses and for his rosy cheeks. Beneath the bombast lay a good heart. And he had a fine intellect, which meant that his periodic arrivals at the Raffles were, in McKie's words, "like the salty tang of a typhoon tearing through an intellectual swamp".

He died in 1938, in circumstances aptly completing the living legend he had become. He himself strenuously denied it in public, but in fact it was true that his bunk on a vessel sailing for Europe—his last resting place, as it turned out—had been widened and strengthened specially to accommodate his imposing girth. Taken ill en route, in Rangoon, he died in some pain at Colombo, Ceylon, but still joking with his nurses.

Beside a figure of such stature, even names like Noel Coward and Somerset Maugham tend to pale in significance. But they were of course two of the hotel's more distinguished guests during these two decades.

Coward was travelling with Jeffery Holmesdale, Lord Amherst, in late 1929, the man he described in his autobiography *Present Indicative* as his "lifelong friend", and who was his inseparable travelling companion in the 1930s. Jeffery had given up a job with *New York World* magazine to meet Noel in Tokyo and do a world trip. Coward had en route finished his play *Private Lives* while in Hongkong. The pair sailed into Singapore aboard a Danish freighter from Siam, Jeffery seriously ill aboard with the amoebic dysentery he had contracted in Indochina. They checked into the Raffles.

Hospitalised in Singapore, Jeffery was ordered to rest up for one month's treatment, so, as Coward put it, they had to be "resigned to this enforced pause in our travels". Coward was hardly in a cheery mood: "During that holiday, I think my spirits reached their lowest ebb on the first evening I spent in Singapore. I sat on the verandah of the hotel, sipping a gin-sling and staring at the muddy sea."

There is no solid evidence that Coward did in fact perform at the Raffles itself, though it is obviously likely, since he stayed there an entire month. Yet he could be quite anti-social, as he himself testified with some relish in describing how, on a sea cruise, he was roped in by a steward for some deck games with certain lady passengers; he resisted, saying he intended to pass most of the day in the lavatory, and that "if Mrs Harrison and Miss Phillips felt like a little Russian bank or backgammon, he could tell them where to find me".

He was promptly ostracised as "snobbish and exclusive", but further disgraced himself as a fancy dress ball judge by awarding the first prize to "a woman who had been ignored by most of the ladies on board, apparently because they suspected her of coloured blood. Had I known this, I should have given her the first prize, even if she had been a Zulu."

Bloody-minded seems to be the word for Coward's mood on this particular trip at least, and so his relatively low profile at the Raffles was perhaps not so surprising.

We do not know where he wrote his famous Empire jingle "Mad dogs and Englishmen go out in the midday sun", but his personal reaction to the oppressive Singapore heat and humidity may well have provoked such a satirical outburst. In his own words, as he sat on the Raffles verandah: "There was a thunderstorm brewing and the airless heat pressed down on my head. I felt as though I were inside a hot cardboard box which was growing rapidly smaller and smaller, until soon I should have to give up all hope of breathing and die of

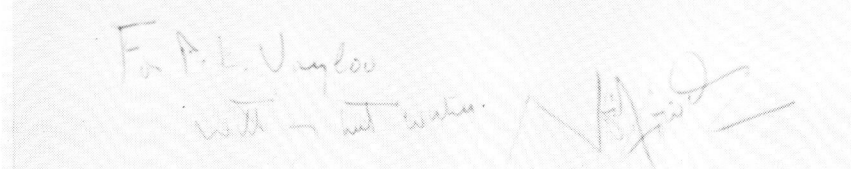

Autographed photo from Noel Coward for hotel staff member Velu (of personnel), whose name Coward has spelled wrongly: "Vaylou" (as it is pronounced).
By courtesy of Roberto Pregarz

suffocation . . . Presently, the thunderstorm broke and raged violently for about an hour. It was the most thorough-going storm I had ever seen."

But heat or no heat, as a result of his decision to "set out and discover what Singapore had to offer in the way of distractions", Coward shortly found himself on stage in the Victoria Theatre, "with large electric punkahs eternally scuffling round and round, while I sweated and ranted in a British warm and full trench equipment", in a temperature he swears was 115 in the shade, playing Stanhope in R. C. Sheriff's moving play set against the First World War, *Journey's End*. Old troupers will out.

Coward had met up with a touring company, The Quaints, then performing in Singapore, and, delighted with this find, had kept them company on their forays into Singapore's slightly stuffy nightlife.

"Some of the more refined social lights of Singapore [probably at Raffles] looked obliquely at us, as though we were not quite the thing," he recalled—"a little too rowdy perhaps, on the common side. I'm sure they were right. Actors always laugh more loudly than other people when they're enjoying themselves, and we laughed most of the time."

His appearance on the Singapore stage was the cause of great local excitement and his name was emblazoned in blue light-bulbs across the Victoria Theatre's facade. But, as he modestly admitted, "the elite of Singapore assembled in white ducks and flowered chiffons and politely watched me take a fine part in a fine play and throw it into the alley".

Coward mentioned the Raffles in passing, in stories such as *Pretty Polly Barlow*, published in 1964, the tale of a young lady who embarks on fulfilment of all her fantasies when her wealthy aunt drops dead at the hotel. He was not over complimentary about the decor, referring to "a mediocre water-colour of a Chinese junk in a lacquered bamboo frame" on the wall of Polly's room, and a "lacquer red wall on which swam different varieties of brightly coloured tropical fish", just off the lobby, probably in the ballroom.

He also described "three American ladies . . . clustered round a glass showcase [in the Raffles lobby] in which were some dubious antiques dominated by a large Buddha made of rose quartz. 'I wouldn't have it in the house if you paid me a thousand dollars', said one of them vehemently . . . 'they bring bad luck to some people just like opals, these Buddhas do, and it's no use trying to tell me they don't. No, thank you!'"

Coward's last visit to the Raffles was to be in 1968, when he stayed in Suite No. 10.

Watching all the variegated characters come and go through the Raffles portals on a number of visits was a distinctly beady pair of eyes—belonging to William Somerset Maugham. Recent revelations have suggested that "Willie" did little of his own scouting for the torrid tales that were to make his literary reputation, leaving it to his travel-mate Gerald Haxton to do the "hard work" chatting up the planters in the bars of hotels like the Raffles, all over the East.

Whatever the truth, Maugham certainly stayed at the Raffles, usually in Suite 78, and said that the hotel stood "for all the fables of the exotic East".

Still on the hotel's list of drinks is the Million Dollar cocktail which was the pride and joy of its fictional creator—Mrs Joyce, in one of Maugham's most passion-packed stories, *The Letter*. In the story, Mrs Joyce is the wife of a lawyer engaged to defend a woman charged with shooting her lover; the real Mrs Joyce was a Mrs Dickinson, also married to a lawyer, and Maugham stayed with them at their home in the 1920s. It was from them that he heard the story of the actual trial in 1911 of a Mrs Proudlock for such a murder in circumstances exactly recalled by the story. The hotel says that it likes tradition, and that this is why they still serve the Million Dollar—a recipe for the cocktail having been handed down from barman to barman.

It seems that two of his books at least, *A Moon and Sixpence* and *Of Human Bondage*, were written in the hotel, mordant stories penned under the travellers' palms in an atmosphere made fragrant by the heady perfumes of frangipani and hibiscus in the Palm Court, directly outside Suite 78. But in Malaya, as broadcaster Giles Playfair said in the 1940s, Maugham really was the "national red rag". The mere mention of his name called forth an avalanche of self-righteous disgust at his "ungentlemanly behaviour," the allegation being that having accepted the hospitality of generous spirited English people in Malaya, he used the secrets of their private lives which somehow he contrived to ferret from them, as material for money-making short stories.

He was unrepentant. When the late Sir Malcolm MacDonald, who had been appointed Commissioner-General for Southeast Asia, lunched with him in London, before leaving for Singapore in 1946, Maugham said: "I envy you, going to Southeast Asia."

"Why?" asked MacDonald, who admitted he then knew very little about the area.

"Because there are more good short stories still to be written in Southeast Asia than any other region of the world", replied Maugham, almost salivating at the thought.

But when he returned in 1959 to the Raffles, he felt the sorrow of an old man only six years from his death. "The Raffles I knew then was nothing like it is today", he said. "The East is a very different world from the one I knew. The people are different. The planters, the government officers and the businessmen who stayed very long stretches here and who, except for infrequent trips, lived the rest of their lives in the East, have all gone. Today, I feel very much a stranger here."

But even then, he could not resist the temptation to "pump" people. Dr Charles Wilson, then Raffles's resident doctor, was called to Suite 78 to tend Maugham's secretary Alan Searle, whose ailment he diagnosed as travel fatigue, requiring a day's rest in bed. Meanwhile, he invited Maugham to dinner and got smartly on the phone to tell his wife that her dinner party for 12 would now be a buffet for 60, not to worry, the catering department would save the day.

Autographed photo of Somerset Maugham given to one of the hotel staff, Ahmad of Reception.
By courtesy of Ahmaed and the Raffles Hotel

"The party really was a success", he recalled later, "We all took cushions and sat on the patio and Somerset Maugham said, 'I would love to hear some Singapore tales'. And out they flowed! From people you never realised had very extraordinary things happen to them. It was when I was driving him back to the hotel that Maugham said that if I didn't write some of the stories down, he would!"

Maugham evidently had not lost his touch. Possibly, he did write those tales down, for according to his roomboy in 1959, Ho Wee How, the author's chair had to be placed in the garden each morning and he would write steadily till lunchtime.

This final visit of Maugham's to his old haunt resulted, as we have already seen, in embarrassment to manager Frans Schutzman. It was a double embarrassment, in fact, for the author was also the cause of Schutzman losing his membership of the Tanglin Club. The pair paid a visit there in each other's company, but were at first refused admission because they were "improperly dressed" according to the conventional formula which required men to endure the heat and humidity wearing jacket and tie. But the Raffles manager, because of his close acquaintance with the club management and staff, was able to talk their way into the premises.

Once inside, Maugham proceeded to abuse the privilege. Staring about him with obvious signs of distaste as he and his companion sipped their drinks, he declared loudly so that the entire assembly could hear him: "Observing these people, I am no longer surprised that there is such a scarcity of domestic servants back home in England." The two were asked to leave and Schutzman received a letter from the club secretary informing him that he was now *persona non grata*.

Another writer, Dr Richard Gordon, author of the popular "Doctor" fiction series, played a naughty practical joke at the Raffles in 1977 when he walked up to the reception desk and asked, poker-faced, if Somerset Maugham was still a guest with them? The exquisitely helpful and polite receptionist carefully checked the current register and said, no, but he would page for Mr Maugham right away. Which he would surely have done, had not manager Roberto Pregarz turned up at this point.

The witty Dr Gordon may or may not know, however, that he himself is the subject of a rather odd Raffles story. A roomboy is alleged to have complained that he was *gila* (crazy). Attempting to take Gordon's shoes away for a routine polishing, he had been leapt upon by the till then supine Gordon, the shoes forcibly snatched from him. Perhaps they had hollow heels, who knows? Or perhaps Gordon had read too many paperbacks about Oriental crime, secret societies and so on—but, a shoe-snatching syndicate?

The post-war decades have seen no less impressive a list of guests, although their style has been progressively less extravagant in this restrained and democratic age. The aristocracy of royal blood was replaced in the 1940s and

Autographs from a book, belonging to the cashier Quek Chua Khoon.
By courtesy of Quek Chua Khoon.

Manager Frans Schutzman (right) with HRH Prince Faisal of Saudi Arabia, at the hotel in 1955.
By courtesy of Frans Schutzman and the Raffles Hotel; taken by the Raffles photographers

1950s by its Hollywood equivalent, the hotel becoming a haunt of movie stars and entertainers. And as international diplomacy became more and more a "jet-setter's" occupation, the Raffles also began to see the passage of more politicians about their serious, sometimes gloomy, business.

The transition sometimes led to confusion. When independent Singapore's first Chief Minister, David Marshall, of Iraqi-Jewish descent, invited Malaya's leader, Tengku Abdul Rahman, to lunch at the Raffles on the occasion of his 1955 election victory, the revered Tengku and his entire entourage turned up in out-of-character, snazzy modern bush shirts. Marshall, however, wore a lounge suit. "My God, Marshall", said the Tengku, "I thought you'd be in that bush shirt of yours again." Nobody was quite sure at this time whether he should be formal in the British style, or casual, according to local observance.

Probably the last of the great "royals" to stay at the Raffles was Prince Faisal of Saudi Arabia, who arrived in 1955, having left the aggressively 'non-aligned' Afro-Asian Conference at Bandung, Indonesia, in some disgust and haste. Frans Schutzman was then the manager. Faisal asked for so many suites for his five-day stay that Schutzman had to "persuade" some other guests to check out, into other hotels. Not having the exact number of suites in the precise configuration requested by Faisal, Schutzman simply knocked some walls down (Faisal had said he would pay) and created four suites overnight.

The Chaplin Brothers in Raffles' Tiffin Room, 1933.
By courtesy of Toyosaturo Ishizu; taken by Nakajima's studio at Raffles

Many whose names are inscribed in the celluloid Hall of Fame have flitted through the corridors of the Raffles—most of them staying in the presidential suite—without leaving much mark other than their signatures in the autograph books so eagerly proffered by admiring staff.

Charlie Chaplin and Paulette Goddard paid visits both before and after the Second World War.

Charlie's arrival in 1930 brought unprecedented acclaim from the usually taciturn rickshaw-pullers. Ordinarily, almost their sole mode of communication with passengers was a series of grunts, but when Charlie, having disembarked from a ship in the port, was spotted by the waiting rickshaw men they almost forgot to compete for his custom on the trip to the Raffles. They broke into a prolonged bout of hand-clapping and shouts of welcome. No one else had ever before been given such a reception. The news of his arrival must have gone ahead, for their only acquaintance with the famous comedian was the flickering pictures they had seen on the screen of a little bow-legged man wearing baggy trousers and bowler hat and carrying a cane. But they recognised him immediately, their faces wreathed in smiles.

Other guests from the film world have been (in chronological order): Mary Pickford; Douglas Fairbanks senior (1938); Jean Simmons; Ava Gardner (pictured in a thigh-split *cheongsam* at the $12,000 luxury suite where she spent

Filmstars Hayley Mills (left) and Trevor Howard (right) during filming of "Pretty Polly" at Raffles, April 1967.
By courtesy of *Straits Times*

VIP's leaving hotel function.
Left to right, Chief Justice Wee Chong Jun, Emperor Haile Selassie of Ethiopia, and Mrs Wee—artist Gerard Henderson's sister.
By courtesy of *Straits Times*

only two nights); William Holden, who liked the special extra-long cigars at the Raffles so much, he ordered 12 boxes during his stay (1954); Marlon Brando (1956); Elizabeth Taylor and Mike Todd (1960); Richard Burton; Ingrid Bergman; Claudia Cardinale (1965); Hayley Mills and Trevor Howard, filming *Pretty Polly* (1967); John Wayne (1975); the producer of *Last Tango in Paris*, Bernardo Bertolucci (1974); and film director Otto Preminger (1976).

From the corridors of power, among guests and diners, the list is just as impressive—in 1940, Prime Minister Nehru of India and, in the 1950s, his daughter, Indira Gandhi, as well as Premier Chou En Lai of China and Senator Robert Kennedy of the USA; in the 1960s, Emperor Haile Selassie of Ethiopia. General Ne Win of Burma, Premier Sato of Japan, Premier Pierre Trudeau of Canada, Kang Kyang Wook, Vice-president of North Korea, Adam Malik, Foreign Minister of Indonesia, President Giuseppe Saragat of Italy and President Benjamin Sheares of Singapore. In happier days, Prince Sihanouk of Cambodia was also a guest and the staff remember his enchanting daughter demonstrating a traditional Cambodian dance from her once-gentle country.

When Sir Harold Wilson, the former British Prime Minister, who was a personal friend of Singapore's premier, Mr Lee Kuan Yew, visited Singapore in 1978, the Raffles staged a birthday party for Lady Wilson's 62nd birthday, January 12.

Present-day guests are often on a private "nostalgia trip"—like Loretta Morrissey Belbach, from New Zealand, an elderly lady who was terribly upset when, in March 1973, she checked into the Raffles to find no mosquito nets. She remembered them from her visit in 1930 and wrote "Where are the beautiful nettings for the bed?" implying she could not bear to sleep in her room without one. Ever ready to please, the management managed to dig up a net for her, although needless to say, in these days of air-conditioning and clean, green modern Singapore, it was utterly redundant.

Another woman insisted only on looking at the Raffles' bathrooms. Why, asked a puzzled management? "My brother was a prisoner of war at Changi Prison in Singapore during the Japanese Occupation. When he was freed, he came to the Raffles, where he had his first bath for three years. He told everyone, 'It was the most beautiful feeling I have ever experienced and one which I shall never forget!'"

And Mrs Susan King of Auckland, New Zealand, flew into Singapore in 1977 clutching six early Raffles Menus in her hand, from the turn of the century, to see the hotel which her grandmother had sketched. Each visit like hers helps Roberto Pregarz lovingly to fit another piece back into the jigsaw of the hotel's history.

Not all the "guests" are invited, or indeed, wanted. In an old building like this, ghost stories naturally abound. One account of a solely "auditory" ghost (heard but not seen), centres on Room 83, in the wing facing Bras Basah Road, which was probably the part added in the Raffles' extension of 1895, incorporating the former American consulate. The story comes from Foo Chian Heng, a Malaysian-Chinese advertising executive living in Kuala Lumpur.

Mr Foo, it should be pointed out, is young, modern, and not at all given to superstition or any interest in the paranormal; indeed, he had to be chased for quite some time before he could be found to tell his tale. In 1974 he had been booked into Room 83 by an American contact who, arriving to collect him the next morning, was surprised to find him entering the hotel shortly after himself. Where had he been? Embarrassed, Mr Foo explained he had stayed the night at a friend's house. Was there something wrong with his room at the Raffles, enquired his anxious friend? Well, yes, there was.

In his own words: "I came back some time after 6.00 pm yesterday. But I felt there was something unusual when I opened the door and I hesitated. I had this tingling feeling at the back of my neck, quite uncomfortable. Anyway, I slid open the partition opening into the bedroom. And then I heard a little girl's voice—maybe she was about eight or ten years old—very young, and English—humming and singing 'Mary had a little lamb.'"

He went into the passageway outside the room, where a maid asked him what was the matter. When he said he was not feeling too good she went off for a whispered consultation with her friends at the service post, and then came back, asking whether perhaps he had had a strange experience?

"I said yes, and told her the whole story. She said there were often things of that kind happening in that room. It was too much for me, so I scooted off and stayed elsewhere!"

So strongly do the maidservants feel about this room, that Roberto Pregarz often has occasion to lecture them very severely about fire hazards when he finds lines of Chinese temple joss-sticks, candles and incense burning all along the passage near Room 83, as offerings to this unquiet spirit.

It seems possible that some ghosts at the hotel may pre-date even the Raffles itself, and be attached to the site. Is this why the Dares's former home was so easy to come by, perhaps a cheap deal for the astute Sarkies, unfettered at first by any formal lease agreement?

Referring to two houses in Beach Road occupied by the Telegraph Company for several years and then by the Beach House Hotel—which is precisely part of the original Raffles—the *Singapore Free Press* reported in January 1886: "There is a curious story connected with the larger house . . . A story got about that it was haunted and it was untenanted for some time. Mr John Purvis senior asked Mr Johnston (then the owner) one day what the price was and he was told there was a limit of $3,000.

"Mr. Purvis asked whether there was anything wrong with it, and Mr Johnston said there was not, except some nonsense about ghosts. So Mr Purvis . . . closed the bargain about 60 years ago for $3,000."

A reader added in the next issue of the paper: "The haunted house on the beach, spoken of in your last number, was tenanted by Mr and Mrs Purvis and after they left, the eccentric Miss Thomas who was well known to old Singaporeans of the period. And after a long vacation, Captain George Julius Dare occupied it and called it Richmond House and again after long vacation, by the telegraph employees . . ." Which, as we now know, is approximately where the Raffles started—not forgetting that little English girls of about eight or ten years of age might well have stayed there from 1871 to about 1877, with the Raffles Girls' School.

Ghosts dating back to 1826, 60 years before these press reports at least, and to 1871? These must surely be the Raffles' longest-staying guests.

And today there are those who obviously believe Maugham still haunts the Raffles. In 1978 a Singaporean schoolgirl and aspiring author, Tham Suet Lan, then aged 18, wrote a short story, *Encounter*, based on an imaginary meeting with Maugham's ghost at the hotel. The spectre advises her: "The secret of successful writing is you have to believe in what you write", adding for good measure, "It takes courage not to be a little grey man in a dismally grey world."

9 EPICUREAN FOOD AND DRINK

Food and drink have been strong points at the Raffles from the very beginning, and today the menus and wine lists in the celebrated Elizabethan Grill and Tiffin Room cater for the tastes of gourmet and gourmand alike.

It was something of a triumph to produce a decent meal in Singapore even well into the twentieth century, for there was no proper refrigeration before the 1930s to combat the dank heat, in which temperatures are in the thirties Centigrade, and humidity ranges as high as 90 percent. Until 1934 the Raffles purchased huge quantities of ice from ice factories and stacked up its food in a storeroom. Then cold storage helped to modernise its refrigeration rooms.

Very little food can stay fresh for more than a few hours in such a climate; the slightest trace of sugar left exposed will attract hordes of ants and not a few cockroaches, even in the most "civilised" of homes. Deadly tropical diseases, all manner of exotic dysenteries, cholera and typhoid, were endemic in swampy Singapore and would still surface even today were the ever-vigilant health authorities to turn their backs for so much as a second. Only in very recent decades has it been safe to drink unboiled tap water.

Meat was therefore always imported live. There were plentiful local supplies of fish, chickens and ducks.

On top of problems caused by the climate, there was at first no electricity or piped gas for cooking—the huge brick ovens were largely wood-fuelled, a process that accelerated the clearance of wooded and swamp areas in Singapore.

As a result, one opted either for the local curries, whose fragrance and spiciness disguised any shortcomings, and possibly neutralised their accompanying dangers, or ended up eating mediocre imitation English cuisine.

However much the food left to be desired, it seems hardly to have prevented the Europeans in early Singapore from eating in a manner more suited to a carbohydrate-starved Sherpa trying to keep warm in the Himalayas, than the indolent rich in weather like Singapore's, where you perspire just sitting still.

The routine around the turn of the century went something like this, for the men at least: after a ride or walk early in the morning, a cup of tea and biscuits while reading or writing letters, before a 9.00 am breakfast of fish, curry and two eggs washed down with a tumbler of claret (at which time the ladies made their first appearance of the day); after visits in town and some office work, a 1.00 pm "tiffin" of curry and rice, fruit or biscuits, with a glass of beer or claret; after some business gossip in the afternoon, followed by sports before sundown, at about 5.00 pm, a sherry and bitters at about 6.00 pm; dinner was at 6.30–7.00 pm, regular as clockwork at the same time every day, and consisted of soup, fish, beef/mutton/turkey or capon, with tongue, fowl cutlets and vegetable side dishes, curry, rice and *sambals*, the delicious tit-bits—pickles and the like—that

EPICUREAN FOOD AND DRINK

Replica of an 1899 Menu.
Produced by the hotel on its 90th anniversary, from an original showing the 10-course breakfast then available. As the hotel commented in 1977, "The price is regrettably changed!"
By courtesy of Roberto Pregarz and the Raffles Hotel

go with local curries, finished up with dessert, cheese and fruit together with beer and sherry, at which point the ladies would leave the men to their cigars.

By 9.00 or 10.00 pm, everybody had gone to sleep, perhaps understandably, considering the weight on their bellies.

This way of life was observed at this time at the Raffles, for it must be remembered that most of its guests in those days were long-stay or permanent guests, residents of Singapore who followed the local lifestyle, not itinerant tourists. Consequently, the popular penchant for gourmandise was pampered by the management. The Bill of Fare for breakfast in 1899 was daunting indeed: porridge, fried fish, mutton chops, devilled fish, cold beef and salad, boiled eggs, cheese, fruits, tea and coffee, after consuming which you were counselled to down a glass of Benedictine, which would "facilitate the digestion". One would certainly hope so.

A Criterion dinner menu of 1900 offered canapés of *paté de foie gras, printaniere d'Orleans* soup, *bouchées des dames à la Dubarry*, followed by the fish course, *paupiettes de rouget a la Joinville* with *pommes dauphine*, and then *filet de boeuf à la Richelieu*. For entrées, *ortolans à la financière* and *suprême de chapon à la Toulouse*. The high-sounding Gallic names however kept company with old English favourites such as roast turkey with cranberry sauce, lettuce with mayonnaise and Brussels sprouts, asparagus, young green peas and green beans. For afters, if you were still not prostrate, there were *tutti-frutti* ice cream, *petits fours armandines*, cheese, fruit and coffee.

In 1905 the hotel advertised its "largest marble dining hall in the East" and, in even larger, bolder letters, "Cuisine The Best—this department is under the immediate supervision of two European chefs," implying that this was then the sole guarantee of both quality and safety.

No discerning tourist would now dream of leaving Singapore without tasting some local delicacies cooked by locals, but in the old days Europeans mostly avoided them unless their provenance had been established beyond all reasonable doubt. Unfortunately, there are those timid souls even now who feel the same way, especially if faced with a tasty bowl of soup with whole chicken's feet—skin, gristle and all—floating in it, or if offered a choice morsel of sea-slug, jelly-fish, or even the greatest treat of all, the eye of the fish in a fish-head curry.

Just down the road from the Raffles is the heart of Singapore's Chinatown, where you can eat just about anything you want, as well as an awful lot you very possibly may not want, from turtles freshly dragged screaming from their shells, to snakes and mice. By the 1920s local Chinese cooks had been trained in the gentle arts of European cuisine and comfortable, full-bellied Singapore began to devise ever more opulent feasts.

Noel Coward rather unkindly attributed the sudden collapse and death of one of his characters—the wealthy but unlovable Mrs Innes-Hook, in *Pretty Polly Barlow*—to having "stuffed herself with curry at the Raffles . . . three large gin slings before lunch and an enormous plate of prawn curry at lunch".

But our friend whom we met in the last chapter. the legendary archaeologist

Professor Pieter van Stein Callenfels, was equal to any hotel menu. When a friend wagered a case of the best champagne that he could not eat every dish on the menu at another hotel, he not only won the bet but immediately consumed every course again, in reverse order "just to show that I can do it". And then he drank a bottle of schnapps to whet his appetite for the next meal.

On another occasion, when five of Callenfels' friends failed to turn up for their curry tiffin, he ate for six anyway.

One can almost imagine the wretched Raffles food and beverage manager of the time making feverish preparations, ordering twice his normal quantities the minute he was informed of Callenfels's imminent arrival.

Almost as extraordinary was a long-stay Australian guest in the 1950s, a mining executive from Broken Hill, who, according to ex-manager Frans Schutzman, insisted on eating lamb chops for breakfast, lunch and dinner, and could not be persuaded to try anything else.

After the war, it was political independence for Singapore that most

Italian Wines

No.		Vintage	Bottle
			$ cts.
25	Chianti		3 50

White Bordeaux

26	Chateau Yquem	1924	12 00
27	Sauternes		3 50
28	Barsac		3 50
29	Graves		3 50

White Burgundy

30	Chablis		5 00

Hocks

31	Riesling	1929	5 50
32	Hochheimer	1928	4 50
33	Liebfraumilch	1933	4 50
34	Rudesheimer	1933	3 50
35	Niersteiner	1933	3 00

Moselles

36	Berncastle Moselle		5 50
37	Zeltinger Schlossberg	1933	—
38	Zeltinger	1933	3 00
39	Zeltinger (Deinhard)		3 00

1937 Wine List from Raffles. The prices certainly look dated (there are approximately 14 Singapore dollars to the pound sterling, 1981). By courtesy of Ray Tyers and the Raffles Hotel

transformed the standard Raffles menu, although regular Scandinavian *smørgasbrød*, or open-sandwich, lunches created a momentary diversion in the 1950s.

Since then, the kitchen's repertoire has blossomed with the grafting of local specialities and inspired East–West hybrids, Raffles' own invention, on to old English standby dishes like roast beef, and the Italian classics that have been served for so long in the hotel.

For those who should know best, the Raffles' table is, rightly or wrongly, remembered as a criterion against which all Asian cooking can be measured. Reviewing a London restaurant in 1977, *Punch* magazine pronounced a thumbs down for the *crème brulèe* but reassured the would-be diner with "but not to worry, the sweet scent of Raffles Hotel hung in the air". And Craig Claiborne, the *New York Times* gourmet writer, said in 1974, "In our book, Raffles is chief among the very few tourist attractions Singapore offers. If you haven't dined at Raffles, you haven't been to Singapore."

Naturally enough, Raffles cashes in on its history wherever possible, and menus are replete with improbably-named dishes such as *Consommé Kipling, Paupiette de Rouget Maugham, Suprême de Capon Raffles* or *Ananas Surprise Tumasek* (the old Malay name for Singapore).

There are still attractive colonial food options open to the visitor: notably traditional afternoon tea, in true English style, in the airy Tiffin Room, a meal consisting of delicately cut finger sandwiches (cucumber, à la Oscar Wilde—of course), hot curry puffs (an Anglo-Indian *makan kechil* as the Malays would call it, or tit-bit snack, a little bit like the English hot meat "Cornish pasty", but with spicy meat-and-vegetables filling encased in the fluffiest flaky pastry), cream cakes and tea from the Cameron Highlands in Malaysia, from Ceylon or from China—jasmine or chrysanthemum.

And there is, of course, tiffin itself, the original curry lunch spread, with fish, eggs, beef, chicken, vegetables, all dizzingly aromatic, some swimming in dark red, hot chilli-based sauces, others dry-fried and piquant, and yet others dotted with fragments of cinnamon, coriander, cardamom and clove, speckled with mustard seed, and tinted with the deep yellows of turmeric or saffron. The palate is further titillated by sweet and sour mango pickles, salty dry-fried *ikan bilis* (a tiny sprat-like fish), Malay prawn *keropok* (crisp, freshly-fried prawn-flavoured crackers), chopped cucumber and tomato, flaked fresh coconut (another locally grown product), crispy onion chips, the sharply tangy raw-vegetable pickle *achar*, and a host of other accompanying *sambals*.

The cuisine of the British Empire, in other words, is now available to anyone who stays at the Raffles. In the Tiffin Room, that original "marble hall" with its Cathedral-like skylight roof, overlooked by two tiers of arcaded galleries and ceiling fans still whirring above the huge potted plants interspersing serried ranks of simple white rattan chairs, the tables laid with the exotic batik-print cloths for which Malaya is so well known, it is possible to step back to the turn of the century.

In the somewhat laboured "Tudor" decor of the Elizabethan Grill—right down to leaded windows garnished with wrought-iron Tudor roses, and complete with pompous portraits of Elizabeth I and Winston Churchill, chintzy furnishings and wallpaper, wood-panelling and tasselled lampshades—the gourmet is exposed to astounding culinary variety.

Besides such staples as the Anglo-Indian mulligatawny soup (the name aptly is a corruption of the Indian for "pepper water"), prime rib of beef served on the superb pre-war silver trolley, lamb chops, apple pie and the like, there are also French classics such as *pâté de foie gras*, lobster *bisque, steak au poivre, sole meunière* and *crêpes suzette*. The occasional oddball dish like *bortsch smatana* also crops up. Thanks to the Italian Connection, there is a strong Italian element—*antipasto, prosciutto, minestrone, spaghetti carbonaro* or *bolognaise, noodles Alfredo, ravioli Caruso, cannelloni au gratin,* baked *lasagne,* squid *à la Venitienne, scampi marinara,* beef *piccata pizzaiola* and *cassata Siciliana* ice cream.

Former manager Guido Cevenini's brother Nino left his mark with *Salade Nino*—lima beans, raw onion rings, anchovies, tomatoes, eggs, lettuce, oil and wine-vinegar dressing, salt and pepper.

Singapore's most knowledgeable food reviewer, Violet Oon, herself a "Straits Chinese", drew some interesting comparisons between northern Italian specialities laid on for her at the Raffles in 1975 and Cantonese Chinese favourites, largely because of their shared predilection for garlic. *Peoci marinara*—mussels, or *tua tow* as the Singaporean Chinese call them—done in garlic with parsley and white wine, she pronounced "very local" for instance. Stuffed squid—*sotong* to the local Malay-speaker—with boiled rice, she found equally acceptable to the Singaporean palate.

But what stand out on any Raffles menu and mark it apart from almost any other in the world are of course the strange and familiar names that crop up together in weird combination—local fish such as *ikan kurau* (Indian tassel fish) done "Veronique", *ikan bawal* (pomfret) "Cardinale", *ikan tenggiri* (Spanish mackerel) "Provenzale", and *ikan merah* (red snapper) "Chambertin", for example. Not surprisingly, seafood is a strongpoint for this island nation. The Japanese, finding their own stocks depleted by pollution and over-fishing, are even beginning to import their own national dish—*sashimi*, or raw fish—from Singapore waters. Jumbo king prawns from the surrounding seas are also an attraction.

A distinctive feature of Singapore cooking is the cross-fertilization among several cultures: this makes it harder to find pure, classic Chinese cuisine, or authentic Malay cuisine, for example, although it is generally agreed that the local Indian cooking is better even than that found in the motherland. But the compensation is an array of "syncretic" dishes peculiar to Singapore alone, creative mixtures of Chinese ingredients, such as pork (anathema to the Muslim Malays) and ginger, for instance, and Malay techniques. Such experimentation has led to a completely separate local cuisine, called *Nonya* from the word for the Straits Chinese women who, descended through several generations of Chinese settlers in Malaya, have all but abandoned their "Chineseness", speaking Malay, wearing Malay dress, and cooking like Malays too, but still with a Chinese touch.

The Raffles menu reflects this tradition, as well as providing local specialities such as Indonesian *nasi goreng*, or fried rice, the local Chinese *mah mee*—soupy egg noodles with fresh ginger and garlic, spring onions, bean sprouts, prawns and pork—or *bee hoon*, also known as *mee hoon*, a fine rice vermicelli often laced with pungent chilli sauces, slivers of meat and soy bean curd. The Malay charcoal-barbecued meat-on-sticks, *satay*, is also there, with its accompanying peanut-and-chilli sauce dip.

No discerning diner at the Raffles will mistake the authentic tang of truly fresh pineapple, vitamin C-laden *papaya*, or bananas. There are myriad species and sub-species of locally-grown bananas—sometimes, the bananas are batter-fried, Malay-style, as fritters, or *pisang goreng*, coaxing out their delicate flavour even further.

The sweet-toothed can revel in the raw goodness of unrefined, thick black molasses-like palm sugar mixed with coconut milk and poured over a small sago pudding—*gula malacca*, a classic Malayan dessert.

Possibly Raffles's most daring innovation, strictly for the equally daring diner, is *ikan bawal* fish stuffed with *sambal blachan*—this latter is a thick red paste of *blachan* (virtually putrefied and fermented shrimps) combined with hot red chillies, a tongue-pricker much loved by the Malays. As can be imagined, it is extremely pungent and rich, and apart from its possible effects on the unschooled stomach, has been known to cause temporary skin eruptions in more delicate complexions. Not even all locals can stand *blachan* (which also has a penetrating odour), but for the less faint-hearted, this is a culinary experience definitely to be recommended.

Eating at the Raffles is made all the more pleasant by measured but exquisitely courteous service of the correctly "invisible" type, and an eye for detail—the silverware produced to order by Harrison and Howson, makers of cutlery to the British royal household, the magnificent silver beef trolley, the deep green, tawny orange and ochre batik table linen, the abundance of locally grown orchids, breathtakingly beautiful but in fact as common as daisies in Singapore, and extravagant eccentricities such as huge butter sculptures or ice carvings laboriously executed in the bustling kitchen. Often, these essentially ephemeral artworks will represent a mythical local creature such as the famous Singapore *merlion*, half-lion, half-fish, or other animals considered auspicious by the Chinese, such as the fish, the phoenix or dragon.

These, like the butter pats at your table, nestle on little hills of ice, a reminder that you are still in hot, humid Singapore after all, not the Ritz, Savoy, Dorchester or Waldorf, as you might well have fancied.

Three drinks in particular are for ever linked with the Raffles—the world-famous Singapore Gin Sling created by the hotel's barman Ngiam Tong Boon in the Long Bar some time in 1915, the Million Dollar cocktail mentioned in Somerset Maugham's story, "The Letter," and the One-Five-Oh! created by

Raffles barman Foo Peng Chian in the Tudor Bar off the Elizabethan Grill restaurant, on the occasion of Singapore's 150th anniversary in 1969.

The recipes for all three are included in the appendix to this book. The One-Five-Oh! recipe leaves one wondering whether the "Oh" was an exclamation extracted from the first "guinea-pig" to try the concoction!

The famous trio of "blockbusting" cocktails has been reinforced by two recent rivals, both invented in May 1978 during the shooting of "The Year of the Horse" for the television film series *Hawaii-Five-O*.

Derreck Lee, head barman of the Raffles Lounge, created a new after dinner drink in honour of the wife of Jack Lord, who portrays the character Steve McGarret in the film. Jack himself named it Mint Marie Lord. The colour of the drink was to match a silk blouse worn by Ms Lord in her favourite hue, green.

Robert Ngiam, who presides over the Long Bar, prepared a variation of the Singapore Sling invented by his ancestor for Jack Lord himself. He replaced a gin with vodka and Jack named it the Hawaii-Five-O Sling.

Just as the trencherman feats of Professor Callenfels will pass down to posterity, so will the "drinkmanship" of five visitors who, in 1977, shattered a long-standing record for the number of gin slings consumed at a sitting. Before Roberto's astonished eyes they downed 131, an average of slightly more than 26 each in a space of less than two hours—and had a few other drinks besides. Mr Pregarz's museum, which has already been mentioned, contains his head barman's signed and witnessed testimony to their colossal intake. The five performers were an Englishman, a Scotsman, a Welshman and . . ., no, not two Irishmen, but, perhaps appropriately, two Australians. "I don't know how they did it, because you are liable to feel giddy after just two", was the manager's comment.

10 FACING THE FUTURE

The end of the war brought the Raffles into a race against time: could it catch up with the twentieth century? The immediate post-war years were marked by feverish renovation, considerable sums being spent in particular on the ballroom, which had its gala opening in 1948—the final proof to many that Singapore was back on its feet again.

By 1950 ceilings had been lowered and windows sealed so that modern air-conditioning could be installed in about 40 of the rooms, 17 of which were reserved for air passengers—the VIPs of a time when air travel was still a luxury reserved for the élite.

It was in this year that the go-ahead young banker Tan Chin Tuan joined the board on behalf of the dominant shareholder, the Oversea Chinese Banking Corporation, of which he was the managing director. He was a rising star in both the political and business worlds, and his installation can only have brought the Raffles prestige and new energy.

An important addition to the hotel, "designed for the discriminating" by local architect Seow Eu Jin, was the Elizabethan Grill restaurant, opened on the eve of the coronation of the young Queen Elizabeth II at Westminster on 1 June, 1953. An elaboration of the theme in the existing Tudor Room, it has a mock Elizabethan fireplace—notwithstanding the temperatures outside—leaded Tudor windows, and teak panelling. As the second Elizabethan age dawned, it seemed, the old guard was determined to put on record its determination that everything was going to be the same as it was before the war.

But profits began to dip with the easing of the post-war housing shortage. Both residential and travelling guests were fewer. Other factors were a new corporate tax which came into effect in 1951—which elicited bitter protests from the company's board, particularly as, they claimed, evasions was widespread and collection inefficient—, a rubber slump in 1952 which was said to account for "a slight fall-off in bar receipts", and the gathering of nationalist agitation which culminated in strikes and riots.

It was hard to persuade tourists that Singapore was yet a safe place for a holiday while there was recurrent violence. In March 1950 the Raffles was forced to post security guards all around the hotel after a bomb incident at the Adelphi Hotel, probably the work of guerrillas spilling over from the Malayan emergency, which was then in full swing.

And in December that year the "Maria Hertogh riots" cost 18 lives and resulted in 200 people being injured. Maria Hertogh, a Dutch Eurasian girl whose name was given to the disturbances, had been separated from her interned parents during the Japanese occupation and been brought up as a Muslim by a Malay family. The Singapore Government agreed to hand her back to her parents in Holland, despite the fact that she had by then been married to a Muslim. This was interpreted by the Malays as an anti-Islamic move and in the ensuing street affrays Europeans and Eurasians were subjected to savage attacks.

Beach Road police station, in close proximity to the Raffles, became a small fortress and refugee camp. Visitors arriving at the airport were warned not to go through the centre of the city, and several airlines took their passengers to the Raffles by back street detours. They cannot have had a very enjoyable stay, for there was a dusk to dawn curfew and Beach Road swarmed with British troops armed with rifles and fixed bayonets. Their presence however could not prevent the savage murder of whites, some of whom had been dragged from their cars by mobs, and tossed into street monsoon drains.

Although the sight of military-manned road blocks became commonplace—almost a routine way of life as time passed—the social life at the hotel went on much as before, though perhaps becoming more trivial and aimless. Now post-war disillusionment dictated much of the behaviour of the clientele and the rage was fashion shows, beauty parades, ballroom dancing competitions and variety extravaganzas, some but by no means all to raise funds for charity.

People dived in fountains, donned fancy dress; it was the "silly season" of Singapore's history, awash with euphoria. Jovial master of ceremonies Johnny Johnson, who was an expert coral-diver when not being the "life and soul of the party" with his lively patter, singing, miming and soft-shoe shuffle, was very much the local "character" even though he had only newly arrived on the scene.

Johnny was painting the pastel water colour lily once to be seen in the Tiffin Room while the Eurasian artist Gerard Henderson was doing the Instant Singapore composite murals in the lobby. "Why can't I do the lobby too?" Johnny asked the manager, Frans Schutzman, in protest. "Because," replied the always elegant Schutzman, "you refuse to wear a shirt while you're painting and it lowers the tone of the hotel." Johnny, who needed the money, went to the tailor to buy a couple of tropical-style linen "Saigon suits". The lady in the yellow *cheongsam* in Henderson's mural is Violet Wee, the first Miss Singapore; the other, seated woman is Henderson's own sister.

The Raffles was still the haunt of the famous, the wealthy and the powerful. It was very stuffy. And very European. This was the era that lives on most vividly in the memories of Singaporeans still alive today: it also accounts in part for the reluctance of some of them to patronise the hotel now.

So real are these memories even in the present more enlightened times that older inhabitants of the city who became politically conscious in the 1950s still feel uncomfortable. Typical of their attitude was that of a local friend of the present author who, after receiving a Raffles Hotel postcard from her, said: "I was puzzled at first because I didn't think I had friends in that class." He was showing his age; Raffles is no more symbolic of a particular class today than any of the other of Singapore's hotels, the more modern of which the average resident is delighted to frequent.

The army remained very much a presence, even after the British military

Raffles Hotel today.
View of the Tiffin Room from 1st floor airwell gallery.
From the author's collection.

RECOMMENDED FOR THE FORCES

THE RAFFLES HOTEL, BEACH ROAD   HAS BEEN APPROVED FOR THE PATRONAGE OF MEMBERS OF HER MAJESTY'S FORCES

R Walle

COMMISSIONED MASTER AT ARMS. NAVAL PROVOST MARSHAL | MAJOR DEPUTY ASSISTANT PROVOST MARSHAL, SINGAPORE BASE DISTRICT | SQUADRON LEADER DEPUTY ASSISTANT PROVOST MARSHAL, No. 31 R.A.F. POLICE DISTRICT (SINGAPORE)

DATE

Army Patronage became more important to the Raffles post-war in the 1950s, after a history of snobbery, not admitting anyone but the highest-ranking officers.
By courtesy of Roberto Pregarz and the Raffles Hotel

administration had completed its post-war reorganisation in 1946. With it had come a host of entertainers to distract the troops, many of whom were billeted at the Raffles, and slowly the old stiff social barriers were broken down. The management relaxed its former rules, realising at least on which side its financial bread was buttered. Ignoring the contempt of senior officers of the "Old Guard", the hotel encouraged servicemen to patronise it, offering them special concessions on certain nights. This must have drawn many a wry smile from men like former Gunner Russell Braddon who remembered being unceremoniously ordered out.

Possibly it was when a "personage" such as Mr (later Sir) Malcolm MacDonald, Commissioner-General for South-east Asia in the 1950s, made plain his dislike for outworn, snobbish conventions that bastions of the colonial age woke up completely to the fact that times were changing rather more quickly than might be comfortable. MacDonald, son of Ramsay MacDonald, the pre-war Labour Prime Minister, scorned the old customs. "There was still a lot of racism in Singapore, which I resented," he recalled later. He refused to become a patron of the "whites only" Tanglin Club and felt similarly that it would be compromising to frequent the Raffles more than strictly necessary.

He also led a revolt against what was considered proper dress, especially in "posh" places. Day dress had already progressed from the conventional white *tutup* suit to "planter dress"—dark blue shorts known as "*dhoby* dodgers", worn with a short-sleeved shirt that hung loose outside the shirt, and long socks. But dinner and dances were still full-dress affairs, at the Raffles as elsewhere, and MacDonald scandalised the colony when he proposed the royal toast at a cocktail party wearing shirt and trousers with cummerbund but no jacket or tie. He would also appear clad in a simple open-neck shirt made of Malayan batik, the exotic, wax-printed cloth used by the Malays for their traditional sarongs. This garb remains smart cocktail wear for men today in Malaysia, although it is less common in Singapore. Sensing the new mood among the populace as the cry of *Merdeka*! (Freedom) rang out louder and louder, the Raffles hurriedly brought in some local colour in the form of its Malayan night cultural shows, which are still popular with tourists today.

When the People's Action Party swept to power in the 1959 elections the hearts of most expatriates and local businessmen were filled with foreboding: the party

The Raffles ballroom and Long Bar, 1954.
By courtesy of Frans Schutzman and the Raffles Hotel; taken by the Raffles photographers

Inset. The Long Bar in the 1970s.
By courtesy of Roberto Pregarz and the Raffles Hotel; taken by the Raffles photographers

was at that time identified with militant street campaigns and a basically anti-western ideology. The Raffles Board, chaired by Tan Chin Tuan, who had been formerly active in an opposition party, went into a huddle.

Suddenly the Elizabethan Grill, which had so recently been the hotel's showpiece and symbol of the *Baba* Chinese loyalty to the British Crown, was renamed the Epicurean Grill, lest the royalist association of the old name incur the ire of the new rulers. Queen Elizabeth II's portrait, by Gerard Henderson, was tactfully removed from the restaurant walls and put into storage. But this dethronement misfired. The main users of the grill happened to be the British business community, who promptly boycotted the place. As one habitué cynically put it, "all the expense accounts went away".

The apprehensive mood did not last long, however. At first it may have been the loss of the expense accounts that persuaded the management to restore the old name. This was after the lapse of four months and the publication of a letter of complaint in the London *Times*. But the Queen's portrait has never been returned and to this day there is a painfully obvious gap on the wall since both Henderson's painting of the Tudor Queen Elizabeth I and one of Second World War statesman Sir Winston Churchill still hang there. The Churchill painting was donated by Singapore artist Mr S. Darn-Kenth as late as 1978: colonial sympathies, it seems, linger on although the present day business community of all colours and creeds are virtually unanimous in their admiration of the way in which the new administration has performed its task.

Singapore began to prove its social, economic and political stability after its forcible separation from Malaya in 1965. The tourist cake certainly became larger, but it was touch and go whether the Raffles's slice would grow proportionately. Apart from competition with other hotels for custom, there was also keen competition for the services of trained staff. The total pool was very limited and Raffles's team of experienced "boys" became human hunting trophies for the new hotels and catering establishments which were springing up.

Yet profits nearly doubled, from nearly $400,000 in 1966 to $700,000 in 1970. The hotel shares set into the trading pattern for which they are still known—inactive but profitable, and probably substantially under-valued, in terms of book-valued assets. Everyone wants to hang on to his Raffles Hotel shares. Increasingly however trading profits, reflecting the competition in a dynamic hotel and restaurant sector of the economy, have been eclipsed by the income from the hotel's plump investment portfolio. In 1967 Raffles Hotel Ltd formed a new subsidiary, Raffles Hotel (Singapore) Ltd, to hold some of the investments previously handled by New Raffles Hotel Ltd. Ominously, Tan Chin Tuan said that financial reserves were being conserved against a time when it might be necessary to rebuild or replace the hotel.

As competition continued to grow still further in 1972, board chairman Charles Tresise soothed shareholders' fears with a confident assertion that the Raffles would "continue to attract discriminating guests who require more than the stereotyped accommodation in modern hotels". One-time manager Charles

Raffles Hotel today
Above, left:
Booming, developing Singapore looms tall behind the old Raffles Palm Court.
Above, right:
Swimming pool in the corner of the Palm Court.
Below, left:
View of one of the wings flanking the Palm Court, from the first floor.
Below, right:
Gracious arches typical of the Sarkies' taste still adorn the Raffles.
All from the author's collection

Dorkins repeated this sentiment the same year when he said: "If you look at one of the new hotels now, it's all glitter and glass, but what will it be like in five years? The gilt will have worn off. I would say that a number of new hotels will close down, but not Raffles. Raffles will carry on."

Such reassurances were necessary at the time, for there were rumours that the hotel would be demolished ere long. "It's nonsense", fumed the incensed Mr Dorkins. But there were plenty of vultures lurking in the wings: only in 1969, McCulloch Properties Inc of California had written to manager Mario Marchesi proposing to incorporate a "Raffles Hotel" in their new city at Lake Havasu, Arizona, alongside the actual London Bridge they had already bought from the City Corporation of London. It was a toss-up whether this would be the real Raffles or an imitation.

Only the realisation that the hotel's main asset was its age pulled it back from the edge of disaster in the early 1970s, when it was quite common for as many as 115 of the 127 suites (really, there are no "rooms") to be empty. The promotion of the Raffles as a historic monument owes much to the prescience of the present manager. Mr Pregarz was quick to realise that the way to restore former glories was to invest in the past and capitalise on the romantic tradition that clung to the name Raffles.

Raffles Hotel today.
The front entrance on Beach Road, still where the Japanese occupiers located it.
By courtesy of the Raffles Hotel; taken by the Raffles Photographers

Raffles Hotel today.
The old rickshaw pullers always found the hotel a profitable "pitch"—so do today's last remaining trishaw-riders. They wait outside the Beach Road front entrance for tourists.
From the author's collection

The right formula had been found. Trading profits soared to around the $1 million mark and the occupancy rate to 90 percent. The hotel is now a must to all seeking the atmosphere of the days when Maugham cruelly dissected the circumscribed, inward-looking lives of the Empire builders who brought Victorian mores from a cold climate to a lush, tropical land.

Raffles today is just as much a magnet as it was in those far-off times to authors, journalists and entertainers—there is a "Writer's Bar" just off the Elizabethan Grill to celebrate the fact and a local play and poetry-reading group "The Raffles Group" has based itself at the hotel. Films for cinema and television, fiction as well as documentary, are shot almost weekly in the hotel and it pops up regularly in the world's newspapers and magazines, swelling the manager's already bursting scrapbooks. The American news agency, United Press International, maintains its office in a hotel suite, as does a Singapore film company of Australian origin, Filmwest, which has also made a light-hearted film history of the hotel. The Foreign Correspondents' Association of South-east Asia also bases itself at the hotel and The Writer's Bar regularly buzzes with tall tales and gossip of the kind Maugham would have adored.

Even tourists who are not numbered among the 6000 guests who on average stay there each month, come by the coachload just to sample a Singapore Sling and hear Roberto Pregarz's clever tape-recorded dramatised commentary on the hotel's history, which is also available in the audio-visual form, with illustrative slides, in the Tiffin Room, following Singapore's latest media trend, a fad for audio-visual presentations.

Ghosts, as we have seen, walk the rambling passages and whisper amid the wood panelling; the walls are hung with photos and drawings of scenes and people of the past. At the back of the Tiffin Room, the old Victorian billiards table and scoreboard still sit neglected. It is still possible to come across gloriously uneconomic empty spaces on spacious landings, with nobody in sight.

But Singapore today is a dynamic place and, outside the hotel, nothing has stood still. Answering a concerned American romantic who in 1973 enquired what was to be the Raffles' fate, Prime Minister Lee Kuan Yew, very much a moderniser himself, said at a Washington press conference:

"Well, it is there. People go back for a touch of Somerset Maugham and travellers' palms are there, the atmosphere is there, but around it, it is fast disappearing . . . I think we have marked out certain areas where we hope to keep just that little reminder of what it used to be, so that there will be a sense of continuity . . . You have got to decide how much of the old to retain and how much you have got to live in and build for tomorrow."

A breath-taking $750-million (Singapore dollars) project, the Raffles City is now underway, scheduled for completion in 1986, just about the hotel's Centenary year. The details seem to shift from day to day, but it is certain that the "City" will be a vast hotel-shop-office complex, incorporating probably a 66-storey tower, a huge convention hall, a 42-storey office block and a gigantic shopping arcade. Where does this leave the Raffles Hotel, comparatively

Lilliputian amid these galumphing Gullivers? Rumbles of protest were heard again in June 1980 but, sadly, they came as usual, from foreigners.

An Anglo-American committee of financiers led by Mr Robert Mayall, a New York investor, announced their intention of doing all they could to save this "living museum" from what looked like imminent destruction; if necessary, they would buy it over. They estimated its value at up to US$50 million.

Singaporeans bridled somewhat at this "interference": they did not need foreigners to teach them what was valuable in their history, they felt. But it must be admitted that Singapore's conservation and preservation record has been dismal over recent decades, during which economic progress has perhaps understandably taken precedence over all else. Now that affluence has been achieved, however, there have been signs of an awakening conscience, particularly among intellectuals, of course: the English-language press, led by the *Straits Times*, has been commendably vocal on all preservation issues, commenting in 1979, in the afternoon daily, *New Nation*, that perhaps soon only a brass plaque would remain to remind passers-by of the existence of the Raffles:

"In another 20 years, perhaps, Singaporeans might start to miss the Raffles. Then it might just dawn on them that something of value has been lost. Maybe it is not part of an Asian culture, maybe it is too colonial a reminder, but it is undoubtedly part of Singapore's history."

Irritating though it may have been, it seems that the group led by Mr Mayall provided just the right catalyst to put an end to all the official dithering about the fate of the hotel. Preservation-lobbyists breathed a sigh of relief in June 1980 when at last a cabinet Minister, the Minister for National Development, Mr Teh Cheang Wan, apparently goaded into a commitment to the hotel's survival, said "The government has no proposal to pull down Raffles Hotel," adding that his planners were studying how best to integrate the hotel into the Raffles City redevelopment.

Further reassurance came, aptly enough, at the ground-breaking ceremony for Raffles City itself, in August 1980, when the Minister for Finance, Mr Hon Sui Sen, said:

"I am grateful that a sense of history has persuaded the shareholders of Raffles Hotel next door, who are also two of the major shareholders in Raffles City, to preserve that august landmark of old Singapore. History may not have been too kind to us had Raffles Hotel met the fate of the old Raffles Institution building." (The beautiful "RI" building, Sir Stamford Raffles' pride and joy, was also once next door to the hotel, but "made way for progress" in 1973).

Raffles City (Pte) Ltd. is the company in charge of the Raffles City project and is 60% owned by Raffles Holdings (Pte) Ltd, a joint venture between the government's Development Bank of Singapore and Temasek Holdings (Pte) Ltd. Among the remaining leading shareholders are Lee Rubber Co. Pte. Ltd. and the Oversea-Chinese Banking Corporation.

The "City" itself will spread over at least 1.0 hectares of land. The scheme has been delayed since about 1969 by escalating building costs, labour shortages and funding problems, but some of the design has already been laid down by the internationally-known American-Chinese architect, Mr I M Pei (who also designed OCBC'S stunning OCBC Centre skyscraper). But now, frantic bulldozing and pile-driving along Bras Basah Road bear witness that Raffles City is at last "on".

Local reports have compared the proposed development in scale and importance with New York's Rockefeller Centre. It will certainly add significant fuel to Singapore's still booming ecomomy, feverish construction being one of the Singapore planners' favourite ways of stimulating economic activity, particularly if a recession is threatening.

Naturally, the project has stirred controversy, both locally and abroad, even in the London *Times* in 1980. Many Raffles fans have faith, one contributor to the *Times*' correspondence commenting, "Raffles Hotel has already learnt, so to speak, to span the ages, and doubtless it will continue, even if over-shadowed by a new complex . . . Singapore was, after all, Raffles' city." Others recalled that Singapore, almost alone among newly-liberated ex-colonies, had been enlightened enough on achieving its independence in 1959, not to topple the statue of its British founder, Sir Stamford Raffles, which still stares over Empress Place into the harbour. Why then should it wish to destroy the Raffles Hotel?

Numerous ideas on the hotel's future role have been floated. It could become a "VIPs-only" hotel, serving foreign dignitaries, visiting royalty and the like. Or it could be offered as part of a special "package tour" to the tourist who wants the modern luxury of the Raffles City hotel accommodation but would also like a couple of days' peek into the historic Raffles Hotel next door.

For those of us who know and love the hotel as she is, it remains only to raise our glasses confidently to a toast only slightly reworded from the one once adopted by brave souls facing the Japanese invaders, "There'll Always Be A Raffles."

RECIPES FROM THE RAFFLES

COCKTAILS

SINGAPORE SLING

One half gin
One quarter cherry brandy
One quarter mixed fruit juices (orange, lime—the small local lime is delicious—or lemon, and pineapple, also fresh and locally grown)
A few drops Cointreau and Benedictine
Dash of Angostura bitters
Top with a cherry and a slice of pineapple

MILLION DOLLAR COCKTAIL

Gin
Sweet and dry vermouth
Egg white
Pineapple juice
Bitters
Decorate with pineapple

ONE-FIVE-OH!

Jamaica rum
French vermouth
Russian vodka
Yellow Chartreuse
Bitters
Lime
Dry ginger ale
Tropical fruit garnish

MINT MARIE LORD

Two-fifths vodka
Two-fifths fresh coconut milk
One-fifth peppermint liqueur
Top with mint leaves for decoration

FROM THE RAFFLES KITCHENS

TRADITIONAL CURRY TIFFIN

TIFFIN is an Anglo-Indian word for light lunch, popularly used in India by the British community to order "A Tiffin Curry Lunch". This custom rapidly spread to the other Far East British outposts, and it was served on Sundays at the clubs. The Raffles upholds tradition. Every Sunday it serves a Tiffin Curry Lunch in the Elizabethan Grill. The difference between the Tiffin Curry and the Indian Curry is that the gravy is not so spicy hot, the chicken is without the skin, and it is served with a large variety of *sambals* (sambals are side dishes in Anglo-Indian curries—usually spicy or piquant).

The Tiffin Curry consists of:
Prawn, chicken, fish, eggs, tomatoes, aubergines each cooked separately in the curry sauce. It is served with white rice and the following sambals:
Peanuts, *ikan bilis* (small white bait or anchovy, usually salted and dry-fried to a crisp), mango chutney, prawn crackers, pineapple, cucumber, tomato, coconut.

At the end, as a dessert, the Raffles serves:
Pineapple and banana fritters
Fresh tropical fruit salad
Gula Malacca dessert
The *Gula Malacca* consists of:
Sago, coconut milk, *Gula malacca* (sugar)

FRESH TURTLE AMONTILLADO SOUP

Gives 8 servings

Ingredients:

Fresh turtle meat (easily available from Singapore Chinatown's markets, where they are dragged live and screaming from their shells)	750 gm.
Water	1.7 litre
Sherry	250 ml
Basil	$\frac{1}{2}$ tsp
Marjoram	$\frac{1}{2}$ tsp
Sage	$\frac{1}{2}$ tsp
Rosemary	$\frac{1}{2}$ tsp
Thyme	$\frac{1}{2}$ tsp
Fresh coriander	30 gm
Bayleaf	1
Peppercorn	10

Procedure:
1. Place all ingredients except turtle meat in a cloth or muslin bag and tie securely.
2. Place all ingredients into stock pot, bring to the boil and simmer till the turtle meat is tender (about 2 to $2\frac{1}{2}$ hours).

3. Remove any scum that may rise to the surface and replace water lost due to evaporation to bring final volume to 1.2 litres.
4. Remove meat and herbs from soup. Throw away herbs and cut meat into small dices.
5. Season soup with salt, bring to the boil, add the meat.
6. To serve, add a teaspoon of sherry per person to the soup.

BROCHETTE OF PRAWNS "RUDYARD KIPLING"

Gives 1 serving

Ingredients:

King prawns (shelled, tail retained and vein removed)	350 gm
Seasoning: salt, pepper	
Hot mango chutney chopped	90 gm
Saffron rice (cooked with saffron and butter	120 gm
Cooking oil	50 ml
Parsley	1 sprig

Procedure:
1. Skewer prawns on to a metal skewer and season with salt, pepper, and if preferred some lemon juice.
2. Fry the prawns in cooking oil till curled and just done. Do not over-cook.
3. Place on bed of saffron rice, heat up mango chutney and pour sauce over prawns.
4. Garnish with a sprig of parsley and serve.

TOURNEDOS SIR STAMFORD RAFFLES

Gives 1 serving

Ingredients:

Prime fillet of beef (this has to be flown fresh to Singapore from abroad)	1 lb (170 gm)
Paté of goose liver	30 gm
Back bacon	2 slices
Chasseur sauce	50 ml

Procedure:
1. Make a pocket in the middle of the beef and stuff the goose liver pate inside. Wrap the slices of bacon to cover round the beef. Secure with tooth-picks.
2. Grill to the degree of cooking required and serve, after removing the tooth-picks, with the *sauce chasseur* on top.

ANANAS SURPRISE

Ingredients:

Ripe pineapple	1 whole one
Kirsch	30 ml
White wine	150 ml
Juice of lemon	1 whole one
Gelatine	25 g
Egg whites	2
Cream	250 ml
Castor sugar	50 g
Maraschino cherries	
Whipped cream	

Procedure:
1. Cut pineapple in half length-wise and remove flesh.
2. Prepare 8 sections, cut into 2 cm cubes, and marinate them in Kirsch.
3. Cut remaining pineapple into small pieces and pulp in an electric blender.
4. Rub through a sieve, add wine and lemon juice.
5. Dissolve gelatine in a little warm water.
6. Beat egg whites and cream (separately) until stiff.
7. Combine the beaten egg whites, cream gelatine and sugar with the pineapple mixture.
8. Pour into pineapple halves.
9. Decorate with maraschino cherries, marinated pineapple cubes and whipped cream when serving.

SELECTIVE BIBLIOGRAPHY

There is no previous work on the Raffles Hotel in existence, although there is a mass of press features almost constituting a Raffles Hotel "folklore". Some of my most valuable sources were of the oral history variety, others no more than passing references in books on other subjects, which nevertheless gave me important leads. Hotel manager Roberto Pregarz's albums were also an invaluable starting point. There were many slight travel guides at the turn of the century, into the 1930s, which were also useful but not particularly readable, as they were virtual listings.

However, here is a small part of the bibliography for this book, selected on the basis of relevance to the hotel or readability for the very general reader:

C M TURNBULL—*A History of Singapore 1819-1975*, OUP, Kuala Lumpur 1977
C B BUCKLEY—*An Anecdotal History of Old Times in Singapore 1819-1867*, Singapore 1902, reprint University of Malaya Press, Kuala Lumpur 1965
A WRIGHT/H A CARTWRIGHT—*Twentieth Century Impressions of British Malaya*, Lloyd's Greater Britain Publishing Company, London 1908
W FELDWICK—*Present Day Impressions of the Far East and Prominent and Progressive Chinese at Home and Abroad*, The Globe Encyclopaedia Company, London 1917
W E MAKEPEACE, ROLAND ST J BRADDELL, G S BROOKE—*One Hundred Years of Singapore* (2 vols), John Murray, London 1921
N B DENNYS—*A Descriptive Dictionary of British Malaya*, London 1894
HORACE BLEACKLEY—*A Tour in Southern Asia, 1925-1926*, John Lane, The Bodley Head Ltd, London 1928
RAY K TYERS—*Singapore Then And Now*, University Education Press, Singapore 1976
NORMAN SHERRY—*Conrad's Eastern World*, Cambridge University Press, 1966
W H READ—*Play and Politics, Reminiscences of Malaya by an Old Resident*, Wells Gardner, Darton & Co, London 1901
J H M ROBSON—*Records and Recollections 1889-1934*, Kyle, Palmer & Co, Kuala Lumpur 1934
J S M RENNIE—*Musings, Mostly Malayan*, Malayan Publishing House, Singapore 1933
EDWIN A BROWN—*Indescreet Memories*, Kelly & Walsh, London 1934
GEORGE BILAINIKIN—*Hail Penang!*, Sampson Low, Marston, 1932
E S ROBERTSON—*Straits Memories*, Singapore 1910
VICTOR PURCELL—*Memoirs of a Malayan Official*, Cassell, London 1965
W SOMERSET MAUGHAM—*A Writer's Notebook*, Heinemann, London 1949; and all his short stories set in Malaya

Noel Coward—*Pretty Polly Barlow*, Heinemann, London 1964; *Present Indicative* (autobiography), Heinemann, London 1937
Russell Braddon—*The Naked Island*, T Werner Laurie Ltd, London 1952 & Pan Books Ltd, London 1955
R C H McKie—*This Was Singapore*, Angus & Robertson, Sydney 1942
R H Bruce Lockhart—*Return to Malaya*, Putnam, London 1936
Ian Morrison—*Malayan Postscript*, Faber & Faber, London 1942
George A Weller—*Singapore is Silent*, Harcourt Brace & Co, New York 1943
Giles Playfair—*Singapore Goes Off The Air*, Books Inc, New York 1943
Noel Barber—*Sinister Twilight*, William Collins 1968, Fontana 1970
Kate Caffrey—*Out in the Midday Sun*, Andre Deutsch Ltd, London 1973
N I Low—*When Singapore was Syonan-to*, Eastern Universities Press, Singapore 1973
Mamoru Shinozaki—*Syonan–My Story*, Asia Pacific Press, Singapore 1975

ACKNOWLEDGEMENTS

The Raffles Hotel trail led me all over the world, to the homes of former, colonial, residents of Singapore, now retired to their homelands, and of a few of the thousands of tourists who have stayed at the hotel. It is therefore almost impossible to mention all who helped me in my three years of research, some of whom are mentioned in the book, others not. But special thanks are due to the following:

RONALD LEGGE, who so wisely trimmed and carefully restructured my somewhat rambling original draft for this, so obviously my first book. It was he who really got the book "off the ground" where it was still floundering after my amateur first draft and my humble thanks are due to him, as well as to my much-taxed but patient publishers.

THE STRAITS TIMES of TIMES ORGANISATION, Singapore, my employer during much of the time that I was researching this book—in particular, the Group Editor-in-Chief, PETER LIM, who so understandingly granted me leave from work on the newspaper when I needed it.

ROBERTO PREGARZ, Manager of the Raffles Hotel, who was my starting point and whose carefully kept, voluminous files on the hotel helped so much.

The many librarians and libraries who helped me:
QUEK YONG HENG at the STRAITS TIMES LIBRARY, Singapore;
JOHN SAMUEL at the NEW STRAITS TIMES LIBRARY, Kuala Lumpur, Malaysia:
MISS G S KHOO, at the PENANG PUBLIC LIBRARY, Penang, Malaysia;
NATIONAL LIBRARY OF SINGAPORE:
NATIONAL ARCHIVES AND RECORDS CENTRE, Singapore;
LIBRARY OF THE NATIONAL UNIVERSITY OF SINGAPORE;
FRANCIS TSENG CHENG KUANG, then Deputy Registrar of Titles, REGISTRY OF LAND TITLES, Singapore;
DONALD SIMPSON at the ROYAL COMMONWEALTH SOCIETY LIBRARY, London;
T G KAY, Superintendent at THE BRITISH LIBRARY, London;

ARSHAK GALSTAUN, President of the Armenian Church, Singapore, who, like all the other Armenians I met during the work on this book, was unstinting with his time, hospitality and friendship, as well as his excellent historical records and old postcard collection. I now account him and his wife Sophie my friends.

ANAND RAGHAVAN who for the first few months of the research acted as my research assistant, while still a final-year student at the National University of Singapore.

RAY TYERS, long-time Singapore resident, author of the valuable and original photo-essay, *Singapore Then and Now*, my good friend, helper and adviser, now resident in Sussex, UK.

JANICE BROWNFOOT, School of Oriental and African Studies postgraduate researcher, London University;
HARRY MILLER, formerly of the *Straits Times*, London:

FRANS SCHUTZMAN, former Raffles Hotel manager, now manager at the Manila Hotel, Manila, Philippines;

MARIO MARCHESI, former Raffles Hotel manager, who sadly died in Rome while this book was being completed;

ERNEST SMITH, former Raffles Hotel assistant manager, now of Dyer and Smith Pte Ltd, Singapore;

ANDREW GILMOUR, formerly of Singapore's colonial civil service, now in Scotland, to whom I am indebted for the identification of the Straits Produce cartoon "Siapa itu?"

DR CHARLES WILSON, formerly of Singapore, now in Devon;

HENRY STONOR, of Trengganu, Malaysia, for almost all the information and photos on the jazz musicians at Raffles;

JOE SPEELMAN, manager of the Selangor Club, Kuala Lumpur, Malaysia, for the remainder of the jazz stories;

MAE and her daughter JESSIE, SARKIES, the last remaining relatives of the original Raffles Sarkies, in Singapore, for their company and photo albums, as well as postcards;

HAROLD and JUAN ASSOCIATES, Singapore, for their skilled and speedy reproduction of countless photos;

DON CHAN, general manager, and LYNDA LIM, his secretary, at the E & O HOTEL, Penang, Malaysia;

KHOO BOO CHIA, curator, PENANG STATE MUSEUM, Penang, Malaysia;

TAN GEOK SWEE, formerly a Raffles cashier, now retired;

QUEK CHUA KHOON, cashier at the Raffles;

ONG CHIN HAI, Nanyang Trading Co, Singapore;

MAMORU SHINOZAKI of Osaka, Japan, formerly Occupation administrator in Singapore;

BORIS LISSANEVITCH and the TIGER TOPS JUNGLE LODGE staff, LISA VAN GRUISEN and UTTARA CREES, in Kathmandu, Nepal;

R B PERKINS, Negeri Sembilan, Malaysia;

HAROLD STEPHENS, freelance journalist sailing the South-east Asian waters;

BRIAN "BUCK" BUCKERIDGE, former fire service chief, Singapore;

DORIS GEDDES, Singapore, who sadly died while this book was being completed;

SIR MALCOLM MACDONALD, former British Commissioner-General in South-east Asia, also deceased during this time;

THAM SUET LAM, Singapore, for her enchanting story on Somerset Maugham's ghost;

THE BRITISH ASSOCIATION OF SINGAPORE and their "BEAM" editor, JOAN BOYLE;

GEORGE PAUL, retired school teacher, Singapore;

GERRY SOLIANO, Singapore;

HAJI KARIM, Sarawak, Malaysia;

ROBERT JEREMIAH, Kuala Lumpur, Malaysia—for his postcards;

H. McGIVERING, Hon Secretary of THE KIPLING SOCIETY, London;

MRS LUCIA BACH, Singapore;

MRS DOROTHY DOWNE, Singapore;

ROY HUDSON, Chiang Mai, Thailand;

MRS SUSAN KING, Papakura, New Zealand, who let me interrupt her fond reunion in transit in the Singapore Airport to collect old menus from her;

MR PAUNCEFFORT, then Head of Chancery, BRITISH EMBASSY, RANGOON,

ACKNOWLEDGEMENTS

Burma, his secretary Mrs B PO BA, and HELEN TAYLOR, formerly at the BRITISH HIGH COMMISSION, SINGAPORE;
HE HAFEEZUR FAHMAN, AMBASSADOR OF PAKISTAN TO BURMA;
JAMES GAGAN, Singapore;
HARRY HOPKIN, London;
G L PEET, Perth, Australia;
JOYCE LEBRA, Professor of Japanese History, University of Colorado, USA:
C M TURNBULL, Reader, Department of History, University of Hongkong, for her wonderful annotated bibliography in her *A History of Singapore 1819*–1975, OUP;
TOYOSABURO ISHIZU of Yokohama, Japan for his photos, especially of Charlie Chaplin in the Tiffin Room;
TAN JOO LAN and FOO CHAN HENG of Kuala Lumpur, Malaysia;
GERARD LEMBEKKER of Amsterdam, Holland;
SIR WILLIAM GOODE, last British governor of Singapore;
LESLIE BLAND, editor, *Wembley Observer*, UK;
JOHN U. TOMLIN, editor, *Middlesex Chronicle*, UK;
A. MILLER, assistant editor, *Evening Argus*, Brighton, UK;
WALLY MARTIN of Perth, Australia;
DR EUGENE LUCAS SARKIES of The Hague, Holland;
N M NAHAPIET of New South Wales, Australia;
W. MACKERTICH of Jakarta, Indonesia;
VICTOR BOLDY of The Hague, Holland;
PROF. RICHARD HOVANNISIAN, University of California;
JAMES H. TASHJIAN, editor, THE ARMENIAN REVIEW, Boston, Massachusetts, USA;
BILL TALANIAN, California, USA;
SHUNJI TAOKA, Defence Correspondent, *Asahi Shimbun*, Tokyo;
JUDD KINNE, Singapore, for leading me to a ghost story;
LIM KIM GUAN, Singapore tourist guide, for his generous background notes and considerable personal knowledge and experience.

Last, but certainly not least, SIVA CHOY, my best friend, without whom it would all have got done so much sooner.

The author would like to acknowledge the following for permission to quote from published sources:
John Farquarson Ltd for an extract from *The Naked Island* by Russell Braddon;
Dr Jan Van Loewen Ltd for extracts from *Pretty Polly Barlow* and *Present Indicative* by Noel Coward;
A. P. Watt Ltd for extracts from *A Writer's Notebook* by W. Somerset Maugham;
Cassell Ltd for extracts from *Memoirs of a Malayan Official* by Victor Purcell;
Faber & Faber Ltd for extracts from *Malayan Postscript* by Ian Morrison;
MPH Bookstores, Singapore, for extracts from *Musings, Mostly Malayan*, by J. S. M. Rennie;
Hospitality, Parhran, Australia, for extracts from the article "Frans Schutzman, a Legend in his Own Time";
Sampson Low, Marston & Co for the extract from *Hail, Penang!* by George Bilainikin.